THE TRUTH ABOUT
GETTING MORE DONE

D0110970

Mark Fritz

ISBN-10: 0-13-815048-6
ISBN-13: 978-0-13-815048-8

Pearson Education LTD.
Pearson Education Australia PTY, Limited.
Pearson Education Singapore, Pte. Ltd.
Pearson Education North Asia, Ltd.
Pearson Education Canada, Ltd.
Pearson Educación de Mexico, S.A. de C.V.
Pearson Education—Japan
Pearson Education Malaysia, Pte. Ltd.

Library of Congress Cataloging-in-Publication Data

Fritz, Mark.

The truth about getting more done / Mark Fritz.

p. cm.

Includes bibliographical references.

ISBN 0-13-815048-6 (pbk. : alk. paper) 1. Motivation (Psychology) 2. Self-actualization (Psychology) 3. Self-management (Psychology) 4. Life skills. I. Title.

BF503.F7567 2009

153.8--dc22

2008027518

Vice President, Publisher
Tim Moore

Associate Publisher and Director of Marketing
Amy Neidlinger

Acquisitions Editor
Jennifer Simon

Editorial Assistant
Heather Luciano

Operations Manager/ Development Editor
Gina Kanouse

Digital Marketing Manager
Julie Phifer

Publicity Manager
Laura Czaja

Assistant Marketing Manager
Megan Colvin

Marketing Assistant
Brandon Smith

Cover and Interior Designs
Stuart Jackman,
Dorling Kindersley

Managing Editor
Kristy Hart

Senior Project Editor
Lori Lyons

Design Manager
Sandra Schroeder

Senior Compositor
Gloria Schurick

Proofreader
San Dee Phillips

Manufacturing Buyer
Dan Uhrig

To a very inspirational leader...
Peter Meier

...Someone who understands and lives the
Truths of Getting More Done
and inspires the belief in others that anything is possible.

Preface

"I just don't have the time!" A very common phrase that you probably say quite often and hear others say, as well. The fast pace of life today and the desire to do as much as one can means that you don't always get done what you would have liked to accomplish. However, some people seem to get more done than others, and you never hear them say, "I just don't have the time!" To them, it is never a time problem. Instead, it is about what the time is used to accomplish. How about you?

Time management is a myth. Everyone gets the same amount of time each day, and nobody can really manage time. You cannot use 30 hours today because you are really busy and then use only 18 hours on Friday because you are going to take it easy. It just doesn't work that way. So, you can't manage time, but you can manage how you use it.

Is your goal to get more things done? For some, that seems to be the goal. For the successful people in the world, it is not the complete story. For the successful people, the goal is not just getting things done, but getting the *right* things done.

This book is all about getting the *right* things done.

I've studied how the most successful people get things done, as well as the time-management gurus who have all those techniques to, as they say, manage your time better. I have tried and thrown away many of those time-management techniques and realized that the way to get things done is never about how many of those techniques you know, but keeping a focus on what are the most important things to get done.

This book will convince you, as I have been convinced, that you *cannot* really manage your time, but you *can* manage the focus of how you use your time. You will understand that getting things done comes down to five key factors:

1. **Success**—Knowing what you want provides the reason behind what you want to get done.
2. **Thought**—All action begins in our thoughts first, so thinking is a great way to use your time.

3. **Discipline**—You get things done by disciplining yourself to do what you know you should.

4. **Teamwork**—No one achieves success and gets the *right* things done without the help of others.

5. **Growth**—The more you grow, the more experience you gain to focus on the *right* things.

As you read this book, you too will be convinced that getting things done does not begin with time management, but *FOCUS* management, and then having the *DISCIPLINE* to do what is necessary and when it is necessary. You will no longer tell yourself, "I just don't have the time!" Instead, you will start—from the very day you finish this book—to invest time in determining your *FOCUS* and then reminding yourself of that focus every day—just as other successful people have done.

Here's to you—to getting the *right* things done.

TRUTH

1

It's not about getting things done, it's about success

Life is not about activity, but about accomplishment, and getting the right things done. To create the life you want, start by defining what success really means to you. Defining what success means to you can provide you a focus on how to create the life you would like to live and what you would like to achieve (getting the right things done).

There are many people who go through life not really knowing what they want. In fact, most people would have some difficultly in telling you specifically what they want in life. However, these same people could probably make a very long list of what they don't want. Think about this. If you can really make a long list of what you don't want, you probably do more thinking about what you don't want than what you really do want. Does this sound like you?

To truly be successful and make sure you are getting things done and the *right* things, it is important to invest the time in thinking through exactly what success means to you. Defining what success means to you can help bring your life more meaning and help you channel all your energy into getting the *right* things done. Remember, you can never live your life to it's fullest by living according to someone else's definition of success—not your parents', not your friends'. It is all about what you want, and everything starts with *you defining success for you.*

When you look at defining success, you always need to look at it from a balanced point of view. A great number of people achieve big professional and financial success only to wish later in life that they had made more time to spend with their family and friends. Take a look at both parts of your life, the personal and the professional, and think about what a successful life would look like and what you would like to achieve.

There are two key factors in defining success for you: Your *passion* and your *potential*.

If you were to ask very successful people what was one of the keys to their success, many of them might say the following: "I made a career (or created a business) around my passion." Those who have built their life around their *passion* always get more accomplished and achieve greater success than those who don't.

You can probably see the power behind building a life around your passion, by taking your own life as an example. Don't you feel more inspired and get more energy from doing the things that you are passionate about? Wouldn't you procrastinate less and be much better at getting things done if you were spending more of your time on what you are passionate about versus what you are not? You can see the power behind creating a life around your passion.

The second key factor is your *potential*. Too many people define success based on what they have today and what they might be able to do. The truly successful people always define success based on the full potential that is inside them. Nido Qubein said it best, "The trouble with many plans is that they are based on the way things are now. To be successful, your personal plan must focus on what you want, not what you have." Like so many others, you have great potential inside you to do many things that you would have never thought possible.

Remember, you can never truly reach something that is never defined. The place to start is to invest time in some quality thinking around your passion and your potential, as well as defining what are the things that are most important to you for your life. You are defining success in what you would like to achieve in your life and then designing the life that will make it happen. A great place to start is to just do a little brainstorming on the following and writing your ideas down on paper:

> **Remember, you can never truly reach something that is never defined.**

What...

- ...does the word *success* mean to me?

- ...am I really passionate about?

- ...gives me energy when I am doing it versus taking my energy?

- ...have I always dreamed about accomplishing but haven't really thought about how to do?

- ...potential do I see inside of me and what have others told me about my potential?

The clear WHAT (the success) provides meaning to get the right things done. If you have not done so already, invest the time to...

- Define your passion and what's most important to you.

- Think in terms of your full potential and not just where you are today.

- Define success and design your life—both in what you want to achieve and how to get it.

TRUTH

2

The why needs to be greater than the how

Far too many people go through life just going through the motions. They have developed their daily habits over time, and their habits have become their life. These people have never really taken the time to think about WHAT they want and WHY they want it. How about you?

For you to accomplish what you want in life, the WHY is more important than the HOW. In fact, to achieve the success you want, the WHY always needs to be greater than the HOW.

The WHY is a powerful motivator and is the biggest factor to getting the right things done. Take an example of a person who contracted lung cancer from smoking for many years. The very day this person received the news about the cancer, he just quit smoking, right then. Why? The news of the cancer and the fact that smoking became a life or death issue made the WHY finally big enough to stop smoking— and stop right away. You can see the power behind a big WHY.

You don't always have a life or death situation, but you do have some important things in your life that you want to accomplish. Often you have dreamed about achieving something and have even pictured the end result in your mind. If you kept it only as a dream and you didn't invest any thinking time on the WHY, you probably have not taken much action toward that dream. Also, to achieve that dream, you will most likely need to change what you are currently doing today with your time, and you may even need to create some new habits.

To make the necessary changes or to create the new habits to achieve your dream, you need to build the WHY big enough to take the necessary actions to achieve it. The WHY needs to be big and strong enough for you to change your behaviors and to repeat those behaviors frequently and long enough to put the new necessary habits into your daily life. The example of the WHY, for the person with cancer, shows that a WHY can be powerful enough to change behavior right away.

The WHY is not only important in driving the actions needed to achieve what you want, it can also be a powerful driver of the creativity in you. The bigger the WHY you have behind what you want, the more you make this a focus for you; and the more thinking you will do. The more time thinking about what you want always helps you to see new and better ways to achieve it.

That's the power behind building the WHY. A big and strong WHY creates the need so powerful in your mind (both the conscious and subconscious mind) that you have to have it, and you will do any HOW to get it. When you have to have it, you begin to take the necessary actions to get it. You also begin to not let other feelings stop you. The WHY has then become so strong that you will even do the things you hate to get what you want.

> The more time thinking about what you want always helps you to see new and better ways to achieve it.

The WHY powers the WHAT and gives you energy to do the HOW. This Fredrich Nietzche quote says it all, "He who has the WHY to live can bear with almost any HOW." You see this in many of the most successful athletes. They will say that they often hate the training they have to do, but they love the feeling of winning and being number one. Their WHY of winning and being number one is more powerful than the feelings they get while doing the training they hate.

For your dreams—or for whatever you want to accomplish in your life—the first step is to always build the WHY before starting on the HOW. A big and powerful WHY provides you with the motivation to take the necessary and repeated actions—and to do whatever it takes to achieve what we want.

For whatever you want to accomplish in your life:

- Start by building your WHY today.

- The WHY provides you the drive to do the HOW.

- The WHY always needs to be greater than the HOW.

TRUTH

3

You need to believe it to achieve it

There's a common saying that all of us have said at least once, "I will believe it when I see it." Success in life works in exactly the opposite way. You need to believe that you can have the life you want and accomplish what you want before you will see how to achieve it. The most powerful saying is then, "I will see it when I believe it."

An old story that highlights this very well is about the two shoe salespeople who went to a remote part of Africa. One writes back to headquarters, no one wears shoes here, there's no market. The other one writes back, no one wears shoes here, there's a fantastic market opportunity. Please send me more samples. You can see that the second salesperson had a totally different belief and saw something the other salesperson didn't.

How about you and what you want in your life and what you want to accomplish? If you don't believe you can accomplish what you want and live the life you want, do you think you will see the things that will help you get it?

You can see examples of why it is so important to believe it in the sports world. All of today's best athletes are using visualization techniques to picture running that perfect race, or kicking that game-winning goal into the net. Every time they are visualizing the success in their mind, they are really creating another layer of the belief in their mind that they can do it. The belief that propels them to success in their sport didn't come to them in a flash. It was the constant repeating of that winning visualization that created the belief strong enough in them to carry it out in reality.

You can do the same for yourself. Why not invest time each day and visualize the achievement and the living of the success you want for your life. By doing the same constant repeating of this success visualization, you will build the belief inside you—just as powerful as the successful athletes do.

When you believe it, you then see how you can achieve it and begin taking the actions to get it done.

Belief is so powerful and something that engages not only your conscious mind, but your subconscious mind as well. Let's say that you have defined success for yourself, defined the WHY behind it, and have been creating the layers of belief inside you that you can achieve it. You have created such a clear and powerful target in your mind that your subconscious can also work on achieving success.

Your subconscious mind is really childlike. It works only on what you give it to work on. If you give it a clear and powerful target, it has something clear and powerful to work on.

When you believe it, you then see how you can achieve it, and begin taking the actions to get it done.

Let's take the example of when you bought your last car. You studied the brochure, took the test drive, and fell in love with the idea (the picture) of you owning that car. You were building WHY you needed to buy that car.

By the time you bought that car, the WHY was so big that you would have felt terrible if you didn't buy it. You probably started to notice, as you were driving around at that time, many more cars just like the one you bought. Interesting, but the same number of those types of cars were on the road just months before, but you never noticed them. Why? Because you built the WHY so strong on needing that car that your subconscious mind was pointing them out to you everywhere you drove. You didn't get up in the morning and decide to go look for that type of car all day long, did you? Your subconscious mind pointed them out without you even thinking about it.

The same thing happens when you have a strong belief. Your strong belief becomes such a powerful focus for your subconscious mind to act upon. As you go through your day, your subconscious mind is pointing out people you meet and situations that can help you reach what you want. If you believe strong enough, your subconscious mind will help you see it and achieve it.

You can imagine the power behind building the belief to achieve what you want. The more time you invest in building the belief in getting what you want, the more opportunities you will see to achieve it.

Remember, you can never really see what will create the success for you, if you do not have the belief inside you first. Believe it to see it.

Success doesn't require proof, just belief. Build the belief by...

- Focusing your mind every day on what you want.

- Repeating to yourself why you want it, and why it is important to you.

- Picturing your life as if you already have what you want—visualize it.

TRUTH

4

It's focus management, not time management

No one can manage time. You can't say to yourself that you will be really busy today, and use 30 hours for today; and that tomorrow doesn't look too bad, so 18 hours will do. You cannot manage time. However, you can manage your focus, and your focus determines how you will use your time.

While everyone gets the same amount of time, there are those people who get much more accomplished than others. Why is that? Time is almost never the problem in getting things done. It is how you use your time that is the issue.

There are so many time management ideas, techniques, and software you can use to help you manage your time better. For those who know of the 80/20 rule, 80% of the power behind you getting things done is not about using any of those time-management ideas, techniques, or software. It is about creating and maintaining your focus on what's most important to you and what will move you closer to the success you want to achieve and the life you want to live. It is really about what you decide to use your time for.

How you use your time is based on the choices you make on a daily, hourly, and minute-by-minute basis—what you choose to do and what you choose not to do. How you determine what you say "yes" to and what you say "no" to is what determines what you *can* and *will* accomplish. Your focus is a powerful criteria for determining what you say yes or no to doing. Without a focus, you don't have any criteria as to what should and shouldn't get done.

What really is your focus? Your main focus (or criteria) is based on the success your desire, both in terms of what you want to achieve and the lifestyle you would like to live. This focus helps you determine what you say yes and no to. To achieve the success you defined, you want to focus your time on doing more activities on what takes you closer to success. Most people don't accomplish what they want because they lack this focus. People without a clear focus will often say YES to things that really aren't getting them closer to what they want, and then are always amazed at the end of each day, as they didn't get to do anything that they actually wanted to do. They were actually working to other people's focus and not their own.

Also, remember that your focus is based on what you want (both professionally and personally). You want to make sure that you have the right balance on that focus to ensure you keep the right perspective for the work/life balance that works best for you.

There are many ways to capture your focus so that it can be a constant reminder on how best to use your time. Some people have

To achieve the success you defined, you want to focus your time on doing more activities on what takes you close to success.

post-it notes reminders; others keep a list always in front of them, and yet there are many people who always want to keep it just in their head. The key is to find the best way that works for you, and experience has shown that getting it out of your head and down on paper somewhere is often one of the best ways.

If you are like most others, you will make the right choices on how to use your time if you have a clear focus. Find the way to remind yourself of your FOCUS and then make it a habit. More than any other thing you could do, creating and maintaining your focus will enable you to get more done, and the *right* things done.

Remember, your focus becomes the criteria you use as a daily basis for what you say yes or no to doing. A clear "laser" focus enables you to achieve more of what you want.

Remember, it is not possible to manage time. However, you can manage your focus by...

■ Determining your focus based on the success you desire.

■ Remembering your focus is a always a balance of both your professional and personal lives.

■ Using your focus as your *criteria* for saying either YES or NO.

TRUTH

5

If everything is important, then nothing is important

If everything is important, then everything is at the same level. If everything is at the same level, then there is nothing that is really different—or important. The most important thing for you to do is have a good way of defining what's most important to you. To get the right things done, you need to understand what the most important things that need to get done are—and do those things first.

There's an old story that has been told in many different ways. Here's another version that highlights the power behind a focus and understanding what's important.

A professor brings a large glass jar into class and puts it onto the table in front him. He fills the jar all the way to the top with big rocks, and asks the class "is the jar full?" The class says, "Yes, it looks full to us." Then, the professor pours small pebbles into the jar. The small pebbles fill in between the big rocks all around in the jar, and the professor fills the small pebbles all the way to the top of the jar. Again he asks, "Is the jar full?" This time the class doesn't answer, as they are not sure anymore.

Next, the professor fills the jar with sand. The sand fills in all around the rocks and pebbles, and the professor fills the jar with sand all the way to the top. The professor asks, "Is the jar NOW full?" The class is silent. Finally, the professor begins to pour water into the jar. The water soaks the sand, and he continues to pour water into the jar until the jar is full. Again, the professor asks, "is the jar full?"

In conclusion, he asks the class why he showed this example, and one of the students makes a joke and says, "To show how much you can fit in a jar." The professor says, "That's true, but it also represents what you can fit in your life, when you get the rocks in first."

The ROCKS represent what is *important* in your life and the fact that they need to go into your life first. Taking the example of the jar; would it have been possible for all the big rocks to fit into the jar, if they were put in last and not first (if the sand and water was filled first)? Probably not, and the same is true for your life. If you fill your day with all the things that aren't important (maybe other people's rocks), there will be no room for what is most important to you.

Most people do not invest the time to determine what is most important to them. If you never determine what is important, then everything looks like the same level of importance to you. When everything looks the same, the urgent always seems to get done first. In your own life, if you only did the urgent each day, is it going to get you to what you want (success) and fast enough?

Let's take an example that highlights the power behind doing what's important first.

You have had a busy day, but have been working on what you consider sand, water, other people's rocks, and are feeling a little frustrated. Your partner or friend calls up and asks you to do a couple errands on the way home from work (pick up the dry cleaning, something for dinner, and so on). You have more of what you consider sand and water piled onto your day, and this is frustrating you even more.

Consider a different day. You have been working on the big rocks from the beginning of the day and fitting in all the pebbles, sand, and water around the rocks. You have the feeling of getting things done, the *right* things. Your partner or friend calls up asks the same things, as mentioned earlier, but this time it doesn't frustrate you. Why? Because you put the most important tasks first in your day and you have the feeling of getting done what YOU wanted to get done.

Life is not about just getting things done; it is about getting the *right* things done. Everything you can do to keep the most important tasks in front of you will help you do the important first. Whenever the important tasks are not in your focus, then the urgent and easy to do always seems to get done first. The real key is to always bring the important to the same level as the urgent and easy to do.

Find the way that works best for you, by constantly reviewing your focus for what's important and keep reminding yourself of that focus. The more the important *is* in your focus, the more you will do the important.

> # Life is not about just getting things done; it is about getting the *right* things done.

Put the reminder habits in your life to always make sure you remember what is important by...

- Reviewing your focus constantly to remind yourself what's important.

- Remembering to get the *right* things done is often about what you say NO to.

- Reminding yourself that if everything is important, then really nothing is important.

TRUTH

6

Your clarity of focus drives the action you want

Your focus is what helps you to determine the important from the unimportant. When that focus is crystal clear, it also drives you to take more action on the important, and this helps you to get more done of what you want to get done. With your busy life these days, and with everything that hits you from both a professional and personal perspective, it can be easy for you to lose track of your focus.

Clarity is the key word here because without it, you will never achieve as much as you can. You can see examples of both good and poor clarity in all parts of your life.

If you have children and are explaining something to them, the clearer you are the more likely they will follow what you say and do what you want them to do. How many

Clarity drives achievement. No one accomplishes a vague goal.

times were you in a hurry, didn't take the time to explain something clearly, and then your children did not follow-through and do what you said. It wasn't clear for them and if you had the time to think about it, it probably wouldn't have been clear to you either.

You also see this in the business world every day at the end of meetings. The time has run out and there is such a rush to conclude the meeting quickly and move on to the next one. Someone wraps up with some vague directions on what needs to be done and everyone looks at each other as to ask, "Who really has the action." Another example of things not being clear.

These examples highlight the need for clarity to be good at getting things done, and that clarity always begins with your focus.

Your focus is the criteria by which you say either yes or no to everything that hits you each day. The clearer you focus, the better decisions you will make on what you say yes to and what you say no to, and this results in you doing more of what's important to you. When your focus is not as clear, you have fuzzy criteria to use in making those yes / no decisions. Then, you will likely be saying yes to too many things that are not really that important for you to do.

TRUTH

6

If clarity of your focus is this important, you should put ways into your daily and weekly life to create that clarity and maintain it.

Remember, clarity always helps you to bring to use the power of your subconscious mind as well. The subconscious mind can help you, but only if it gets something clear to work on. The clearer your focus, the more help you get from your subconscious mind to develop those creative ideas and get more. This is why when you go to bed with a clear problem that needs to be solved; you often wake up with the answer. Why? Because you gave your subconscious mind something clear to work on.

Also, the clarity in your focus should always be covering both the WHAT and the WHY. The WHAT are the focus areas that will drive you to complete all the things you need to get done. However, by also focusing on the WHY, you create even more inspiration and energy behind the work needed to complete the tasks. It is always a great idea to cover both the WHAT and WHY for the big things you need to accomplish in your life. They bring both clarity and inspiration to "Get It Done."

Saying yes to something also means saying no to something else. When you constantly keep a clear focus, you will understand much better the trade-offs you are making based on your yes/no decisions. If you feel better about those yes/no decisions, you will have less stress. You will know that what is not getting done is a lower priority for your focus.

Remember, the clarity of your focus drives you to take more action on what you want, versus what others want. Clarity drives achievement. No one accomplishes a vague goal.

Invest the time to make the WHAT and WHY clear for you.

- Continually review your focus for clarity.

- Always cover both the WHAT and the WHY.

- A clear focus drives clear action.

TRUTH

7

Goals make your life self-directed

Having a clear focus is important. However, what gives power to that focus are the goals you create based on your focus. Goals help you keep the direction of your life in line with your focus and create a sense of urgency that drives your daily and weekly actions. Goals put you in the driver's seat of your life. Without them, you are in the passenger seat, back seat, or maybe you are not even in the car.

There's a great way to look at the criteria for the big goals in your life.

Your goals should

- Excite you...and...

- Scare you—at the same time

You will never do something well or have the energy to keep at it unless it gets you excited. Look at defining goals that really excite you, and these are usually around those things about which you are passionate.

Second, your goals should also scare you. Goals should challenge you to grow, and if you already know specifically how to achieve something, it is really not a goal. Instead it is simply an outcome that you have the plan to achieve.

> You will never do something well or have the energy to keep at it unless it gets you excited.

A goal is something that should challenge you to grow and use that potential that is inside you. At the time you create the goal, you probably don't know exactly how you will reach it. When President John Kennedy made the speech about America putting a man on the moon by the end of the decade, it was a goal. Do you think President Kennedy and NASA knew exactly how to do it? Probably not, and for your goals, you probably won't know either. That's the scary part.

What you can also learn from President Kennedy's goal is that he created a time limit. Creating a date associated with your big goals creates a sense of urgency that puts the power and drive behind your daily and weekly actions.

You want to make sure you have a *by when* for each of your goals.

Remember, make sure that your big goals both excite you and scare you, and when you build your life around those goals, you make your life self-directed. These big goals will keep you focused on what you want to achieve and help create the direction your life will take.

To achieve President Kennedy's goal, NASA needed to define some smaller intermediate goals to make sure it could both meet the end of the decade timeline, as well as motivate its people to achieve it. NASA defined some key intermediate goals, and you need to do the same for your big goals.

A few other attributes of goals can help drive you to achieve them.

- **Clarity**—Your goals need to be clear, as you cannot reach a vague goal or get motivated by it. Also, you need to define it in such a way that it is clear to you when it is achieved. The key: If you can't measure achievement, then the goal is not clearly defined.

- **Review**—Goals are not something that are set and then not looked at again for a year. To keep your life self-directed, goals are something that you need to review often, and for some, daily. Goals need to be reviewed often, as this is another way to remind yourself of your focus and what is most important to you. As Brian Tracy says, "The very act of setting goals and writing them down increases your likelihood of achieving them by about 10 times."

Written goals and plans are powerful, as they set both direction and pace, as well as put you into the driver's seat of your life.

Written down goals are like the *Roadmap for Your Life*. Write down your...

- Big goals that both excite and scare you.

- The intermediate goals that will help you progress and motivate you to achieve them.

- How and when you will review them. (Why not daily?)

TRUTH

8

Life is about the journey *and* the destination

There are successful people who had only the destination in their minds. They worked hard, made a great deal of money, and then woke up one day only to ask themselves: Was it worth it? They were singularly focused on what they wanted to achieve (the destination) and forgot that life is also about the journey.

Happiness and fulfillment cannot only be yours when you reach your success and goals, it also has to be there during the journey. Truly happy people have learned to enjoy the journey *and* the destination, as life is about both.

Earl Nightingale said it best when he said, "Success is the progressive realization of a worthy goal or ideal." It is never only about the destination, and a successful life is always defined in terms of both the journey and the destination. If you were to think that you could only be happy when you achieve your goal or reach the success you desire, then you would only be happy for a very short time.

You could say that it is all about designing the life that you would like to live. What would your life look like if you could design it? This is a great question, and if you are like most people, you haven't invested that much time in answering it. So, why not answer it NOW!

You know that it is important to have that target in your mind of what you want to accomplish and what success in your life would look like for you. You also know that understanding your passion and potential are important in defining success for your life. To move forward in designing your life, you want to think about two very important things:

- What makes you happy?
  What relationships, activities, and so on provide you the most enjoyment?

- What helps you to grow?
  What personal development or activities will help your grow (and faster)?

In creating the life you want, it is all about putting into your daily activities more of what makes you happy and helps you grow.

> Remember, you are designing a life that both reaches the destination and enjoys the trip. Invest the time to design your life upfront and you will always enjoy the journey. Jim Rohn said it best, "Learn how to be happy with what you have while you pursue all that you want."

Life is about reaching your potential and enjoying the trip. Make sure you have an enjoyable and rewarding journey by:

- Aligning your life behind your passions and potential.

- Including in your life those activities that make you *happy.*

- Including in your life those activities that help you *grow.*

TRUTH

9

You accomplish more with an outcome focus

Have you noticed people who seem to be busy all the time, but you wonder what they are accomplishing (that is, outcomes)? There's a huge difference between approaching your day and life versus an outcome focus. Those people who choose to have an outcome focus get more done because they are more focused on the what.

The more you take an outcome focus, the clearer the target you have and the more ownership you will take to get it accomplished. Outcomes drive ownership, and ownership drives results.

So, why do people continue to take an activity focus when they know that they could get more done with an outcome focus? As Henry Ford said, "Thinking is the hardest work there is, which is the probable reason so few engage in it." Defining outcomes and using them to drive what you do means you have to invest some quality time to think about the key outcomes that are most important to you.

> **Outcomes drive ownership, and ownership drives results.**

Most people don't invest the time to THINK! Sounds strange, but with the fast pace of life, many people are focused on *doing* activities and don't take the time to think. Also, if you are not thinking, you are constantly doing things out of habit (the same things) and you will always get the same results, unless you change your habits.

The most successful people are the ones who get the most accomplished, and they view their thinking time for deciding the key outcomes they want to accomplish as one of the most important things to put into their day and week first. How about you?

The clearer you define your outcomes, the more creativity will drive you to get it. It is difficult to get creative around a vague target. Therefore, to get more creative and find better and faster ways to achieve your key outcomes, your outcomes have to be defined as clear as possible.

When you have clear outcomes, you get lots of ideas on how to achieve them. The key is to get them out of your head and down on paper. If you just keep them in your head, you might forget them, especially at the time when you could have used the idea to take the *right* action and get it done.

Often a picture of the outcome you are trying to achieve will drive even more creativity. This is why you see many people with pictures of the car they want to buy or the home they want to purchase. With a picture, you drive both your creativity and the motivation inside you to take action and go get it.

Decide today, when and how you will invest time to think about the key outcomes to accomplish what will take you closer to the success and goals that you have defined. The clearer the outcomes you define, the more creativity you will trigger within you, and the more ideas you will get to take action on. Remember, only action is what gets things done, and by defining clear outcomes, you get more of the *right* things done.

It's all about accomplishment, versus just completing activities. Remember...

- For everything, take an outcomes focus.

- Outcomes drive ownership for accomplishment and results.

- Always keep an outcome focus versus an activity focus.

TRUTH

10

Nothing is stopping you but you

The biggest barrier to achieve the success you have defined for your life is never anyone else or the circumstances you encounter. Your biggest barrier is almost always YOU. Your belief in yourself is the only thing that can really stop you from achieving the success you want in your life and getting the right things done to achieve it. Dr. Maxwell Maltz said it best when he said, "Within you right now is the power to do things you never dreamed possible. This power becomes available to you just as soon as you can change your beliefs."

Everything you accomplish starts in your thoughts first. However, what are driving your thoughts are your beliefs about what you think you can do and how you think you should act. These beliefs have been created over time, with many of them originating when you were young. When you were a child, you thought almost anything was possible. As an adult, you seem to have narrowed greatly what you think is possible, and this can be a big factor in limiting what you can accomplish.

> One of the biggest problems with the beliefs you have about yourself is that you have the natural tendency to always search out evidence of your beliefs in your daily life.

Robert H. Schuller said, "The only place where your dream becomes impossible is in your own thinking." What beliefs do you think are stopping you today? What would you do differently if those beliefs were not there or changed to something much more positive about what you could accomplish?

If you thought of the beliefs that are stopping you, the next step is to ask yourself why? You really cannot change your beliefs until you invest the time to really think *why* you think that way. The why will uncover where these beliefs really started for you, and then you can see if there is a strong basis for this belief, or if it grew from something small into what it is today, just by repeating it.

One of the biggest problems with the beliefs you have about yourself is that you have the natural tendency to always search out evidence of your beliefs in your daily life. If you have a belief that you cannot do something, then your mind will always avoid the situation where you might *have* to actually do it. So, the more you are constantly telling yourself that you cannot do certain things, the more you are avoiding those things in your daily life.

These are probably the very things that will take you closer to the success you desire and the goals you have defined, but because your beliefs are telling you that you cannot do it, you are avoiding having to do those things every day.

What's happening is that your beliefs are narrowing down the possible actions you can take to achieve the success you want. The more limiting the beliefs you have, the more you are limiting the actions you will take to get what you want.

Les Brown says, "Sometimes you've got to believe in someone else's belief in you until your own belief kicks in." Often you just don't believe you can do it, but others around you have the belief that you can. It is important to just put your faith in other's belief in you and begin taking action—the action will help develop the belief in yourself to carry it on.

Also, there's a great way to drive you into a new belief. It's called *as if.* Why not just think *as if* you are the person who already has achieved what you originally thought was not possible. When you believe *as if* you are the person already, you will begin to both think and take the actions as that person would.

If you were to think *as if* you were already the person you would like to be, what would you be thinking about today and what are the actions you would be taking?

> The action of thinking *as if* gets you thinking and acting differently than you did five minutes ago.

Whatever you are thinking and whatever actions you think of—write them down immediately. The action of thinking *as if* gets you thinking and acting differently than you did five minutes ago.

To create a different life, you need to begin with your beliefs. Remember, your beliefs drive your thinking, and your thinking drives your actions. Only you can stop you.

Invest time to think through the *why* behind your limiting beliefs.

- Think through what's stopping you from taking action right now.
- *Think as if* and suddenly you will begin taking action *as if.*
- *Only you can ever stop you.*

TRUTH

11

Your past does not have to
equal your future

Many of your beliefs about what you can become or what you can accomplish is based on your past experiences. You probably hit the replay button on your life and often bring up those past bad experiences to remind yourself of what you think you cannot do. Remember, your past does not equal your future, and you and everyone else can only accomplish in the present.

You read stories all the time of people who changed their lives and accomplished great achievements and success. They all had a past that—had it continued the same way— would have held back the person from their achievement and success. However, they believed and you can too—their past did have to equal their future.

> Your past is only something from which you can learn.

Your past is only something from which you can learn. However, if you are like many others, you seem to replay your bad past experiences over and over again. You cannot do any good by replaying past bad experiences, but somehow you keep doing it.

When you learn something from the past, you have something you can use in the future to do things differently and better. In this way, your past can be valuable to you in getting things done. You must learn from it and think about how you apply what you learned to future actions.

Here's the key: Whenever you find yourself replaying a past experience, either bad or good, why not ask yourself this question, "What did I learn from this experience and how can I use it in the future?" This makes your past experiences useful, and you can apply what you learned to do things better in the future.

You will find that when you take what you learned from your past experiences, you will replay those experiences less. Your mind won't see the benefit as much anymore, and the same drive to replay them will no longer be there. Why? Because you learned something from the experience.

There's a great NLP technique that can help you learn from past events, and particularly those that were bad experiences for you. To describe it quickly...you want to replay that particular event in your mind again. However, this time you want to look at it as if you were watching what happened in a movie theater and someone else is playing the part of you. This helps you to take an objective view of what happened. You can also learn easier because you are not mentally in the middle of the event. Instead, you are watching it happen.

When you take what you learned from your past experiences, you will replay those experiences less.

This technique sounds a little strange, and you are probably saying to yourself—could it work? It does! When you watch the event as if you were in a movie theater, the impact of that event on you becomes less. Why? Because you are making it less personal and looking at it as if it were someone else. This objective view helps you to learn from the experience faster.

After you learn from your past bad experiences, forget them and focus on the present.

Remember, you can only accomplish in the present. The past is only useful for learning and applying that to doing a better job in the present. It is what you do today and every day that creates the future you want.

Learn from the past, and focus all your energy on the present. Each day's present becomes your future.

It is what you do today and every day that creates the future you really want.

- Stop replaying your past experiences and focus on the present.

- If you replay any past experience, focus on what you can learn and then move on.

- You can only accomplish in the *present.*

TRUTH

12

The size of your beliefs determines the size of your achievements

Your beliefs drive what you accomplish. Therefore, it goes without saying that the size of your beliefs will drive the size of your accomplishments. There's a great deal of power in that statement, and its impact on what you can accomplish in your life is just as powerful. If you are like most people, your self-belief might not be as big as what you want to accomplish. If what you want to accomplish is greater than your self-belief, then what you want is more of a wish.

Dan Lier, a coach in the U.S., tells a great story that illustrates this concept of the size of your self-belief. Dan was a trainer for a Tony Robbins company and asked one of the successful participants to have breakfast together the next morning. Dan always liked to talk with successful people and learn more about how they became successful.

> You can never accomplish beyond the belief that is inside you.

During the conversation, the successful participant made an interested point to Dan. He said, "I don't really know what you want to do with your life or what you really want to achieve, but I can tell you one thing right now. I don't care how hard you work or what you do. You will never earn $250K-a-year with the $100K-a-year belief system you currently have in your head." That comment hit Dan, and he found it to be absolutely correct. In fact, Dan took what he learned and created the belief he needed to become successful.

The numbers aren't as important as the difference in the numbers. You can never accomplish beyond the belief that is inside you and who controls what you believe? You do. Donald Trump says, "As long as you're going to be thinking anyway, think big."

If you were to study the capabilities and skills of today's MBA graduates from the leading universities, you would find all of them have similar capabilities and skills. So, what will make the difference in future for what each of them will achieve?

If you could read their minds and understood the true beliefs in each of graduate, you would see the difference. The size of the graduates' goals is always limited by the size of their beliefs, and the size of their beliefs is what drives the size of their accomplishments.

Many people invest time and money into their own education but are missing the beliefs that will help them utilize what they learned and achieve what they really want. Take a minute to think about that statement and ask yourself, "Do I have the belief inside me to use the capabilities and skills I have to achieve what I want?"

You see, a belief is really a "sense of certainty." When your beliefs are weak, you have a low sense of certainty that you can achieve what you want. When your beliefs are strong, you have a much higher sense of certainty that you can achieve it.

> Many people invest time and money into their own education, but are missing the beliefs that will help them utilize what they learned and achieve what they really want.

If you have the capability and skills to achieve more than you are achieving today, the problem might be the size of your beliefs—that sense of certainty that you can accomplish it.

You need to continually push the boundaries of your own beliefs—the potential is inside you to accomplish almost anything you want. Your goal should be always to drive your beliefs to the size of your potential. Les Brown sums it up well, "People don't fail because they aim too high and miss, but because they aim too low and hit." Your beliefs will determine your aim and, thus, your achievements.

Your level of success begins with the level of your beliefs. No amount of activity will be enough if the size of your beliefs is not big enough for the success you desire.

- Always start by building the belief to the size of success you desire.

- Aim high and grow your beliefs to achieve it.

- Remember, a belief is a sense of certainty.

TRUTH

13

Your attitude is really your window to the world

Your attitude is something that is completely within your control. When you leave your home each day, the attitude you enter the world with is entirely up to you. Enter the world with a good attitude, and it's like having a crystal clear windshield in your car—you can see everything clearly and far into the distance. Your attitude is your window to your world.

There's a good story that illustrates how your attitude is within your control. An elderly woman was changing retirement homes and was walking down the hallway with one of the attendants from the new home. The attendant was describing the room she would have, including the furnishings, colors of the walls, and the view out the window, and so on. The older woman said, "I'll love it!" The attendant responded, "How can you say that? You haven't even seen the room yet." The elderly woman replied, "My attitude toward the room and life is my choice. It is something I determine ahead of time."

Never let outside circumstances or others determine how you should feel about yourself.

Your attitude is a choice and is something you determine ahead of time. There are far too many people who let consequences or situations drive their attitude. If you are always letting consequences and other people determine your attitude, it is like you are surrendering leadership of your life to others. Never let outside circumstances or others determine how you should feel about yourself.

Sometimes more than any other factor, your attitude can determine what you will accomplish today, as your attitude is what can keep you positive and focused on the task at hand. However, your attitude is something that you can't just take for granted. To keep a positive attitude, you need to constantly keep feeding it positive experiences.

This is why you see many successful people reading the same book over and over again or listening to the same audios repeatedly. There are some successful people who often carry around with them everywhere the book that made the biggest impact on them and changed their life. They are constantly re-reading the book, and every time they read it, they gain even more insight and ideas.

Here are two great outcomes for you to strive for every day:

TRUTH

■ **Be the best you can be**—You know you have a great attitude when you can be the best "you" in any situation. So many people in the world let others determine their attitude for them. Decide to be the best "you" in all situations.

■ **Be the person you would like to be around**—The other key outcome is to be the type of person you would like to be around, as this attitude will always attract others to help you.

No one accomplishes everything they want in life by themselves, and it is always with the help of others. A great attitude is like a magnet and attracts the help of others. When you have a great attitude, you will attract others to help you achieve the goals and outcomes you have defined for your life. Your attitude will determine the opportunities you see.

Your attitude is a choice. Choose to have a good attitude every day.

■ Choose your attitude and don't let others or circumstance determine it for you.

■ Keep your attitude positive and feed it positive experiences daily.

■ Your attitude shapes the way you see your world.

TRUTH

14

All actions begin in your thoughts first

What you accomplish begins in your mind first. You could say that the quality of your thoughts drives the quality of your actions. That being true, you could also say that the more quality thinking time you put into your life, the more you can get done. James Allen said it best, "You are today where your thoughts have brought you; you will be tomorrow where your thoughts take you."

Many people go through life not really investing time in doing any quality thinking. You will always act out of habit if you never invest the time to think. Living a life based on your unchanged habits means that you would be doing the same things over and over again and get the same results.

> **You will always act out of habit if you never invest the time to think.**

If you were to drive your car across the grass, back and forth over the same path, you would begin to create a rut. In fact, this is what you are doing to your own life if you do not invest the time for some quality thinking. Your habits would drive you into a deeper and deeper rut.

To become better at getting the right things done, you need to get better at doing quality thinking. Most people would prefer to avoid thinking as it can be challenging. However, as all your actions begin in your thoughts first, the quality of your thinking can then determine the quality of your actions.

Your thoughts enable you to take on life in a proactive way versus a reactive way. It is important to focus your thinking on what you want to accomplish and not just on what you need to do. This is all about looking at what you need to accomplish with an outcome focus. When you focus your quality thinking on outcomes, you will always have ideas for accomplishing the outcomes with less activity.

Do you have a time of day or times during your week set aside to just think? During these times when you are doing some quality thinking, you will begin to get some ideas on some key outcomes that you want to drive or even some specific actions that you need to take. Don't trust your memory and *do* take the time to write all these ideas down.

The most successful people are always writing down their thoughts, as they know that their thoughts are what are driving their success. The more their thoughts are down on paper, the more possibilities there will be that they will drive action—and isn't action what it is all about?

David Allen, in his book *Getting Things Done: The Art of Stress-Free Productivity*, talks about the need to think in Next Actions. It is often that you think about what you need to do in too vague a way and then never get to take action on your thoughts because of that. Although you are doing your quality thinking and are thinking of some action ideas, it is always good to right then and there, think about the *Next Action* that will move the idea forward. If you catch yourself being too vague about it, then keep asking yourself the question, "What is the next action?" David Allen says that your Next Actions are always something simple—a call, an email, and so on. When you break it down to the simple next action, you will have a much greater chance that you will actually do it.

Decide today how you will invest more time in quality thinking. Set up times in your day and week to do some quality thinking on the key outcomes that will create the success you want. If you make it a habit, you will begin to see a change in your actions, as well. Your quality of thinking will drive the quality of your actions, and what you will ultimately achieve.

Invest the time to do some quality thinking.

- Set aside a specific time during the day to just think.

- Capture down on paper all the ideas you create.

- Determine how to turn those ideas into action right away—The Next Actions.

> **Set up times in your day and week to do some quality thinking on the key outcomes that will create the success you want.**

TRUTH

15

Positive thinking pushes out negative thinking

Positive thinking works and one of the biggest benefits is that when you have more positive thinking in your mind, there's not a great deal of room for any negative thinking. The people who stay positive are good at filtering out the negative input and focusing on the good.

When you are positive, you physically feel much better and you also take more action. However, when you are negative in your thinking, you often find yourself not feeling well and are likely to take less action.

Why is it that the tendency of most people is to think about—often over and over again—the bad things that happen to them versus the good things? All the negative news and what's happening in the world often makes you feel down. However, the majority of your "bad" thinking has nothing to do with the outside world but instead what you manufacture in your mind.

As mentioned earlier, you tend to take less action when you are not feeling positive. If you want to become better at getting things done, think positive.

Sometimes you don't necessarily even need to think positive first. Instead, eliminate the negative thinking from you daily life, and this will allow you to move toward more positive thinking.

If you want to become better at getting things done, think positive.

Jerry Clark, on his program *Think Like a Giant*, talks about a *mental fast*. Jerry suggests that you take a break, a fast, from all the negative news you get from TV and newspapers. Why not take a month and decide to stop watching all the negative news you see on TV and read in the newspapers? It is often the negative input you allow into your mind that consumes your thoughts and doesn't allow the positive thinking to ever enter. By eliminating the negative, and without the negative input going into your brain, you will naturally become more positive. This is a great way of filtering out the bad and focusing on the good.

At the same time, you have more time to invest in your own personal development and read books or listen to audios that will help you grow and stay positive. The most successful people and the ones that are getting things done are constantly feeding their mind positive experiences. They treat these positive experiences as food for success. Just as you would not last long without nutritional food, successful people feel that their success will not last forever unless they are constantly feeding themselves positive experiences—continuing to inspire their action.

Staying positive and motivated is not something that you can take for granted. Your personal development and filling your mind with positive readings is not something you can do just once in a while. To stay consistently positive, you need to fill your mind with the positives daily.

Remember, it is all about filling your mind with positive input. This comes from what you read, what you listen to, and the people you spend your time with. When you fill your mind with positive input and begin to think more positive thoughts, you will not have any room for negative thoughts.

Strive to fill you mind with the positive, and you will find yourself with more motivation each day to take the necessary actions and accomplish what you want in your life.

Stay positive and keep yourself in the best mindset for action.

- Push out negative thinking by filling your mind with positive input and experiences.

- Positive thinking fuels your motivation to take more action.

- There's never any room for negative thinking if you constantly fill your mind with the positive.

TRUTH

16

What you learn only has power when put into action

You can never learn enough in your life if you just rely on your own experiences. What you read, listen to, and the people you meet can have a big impact on what you learn and what you are then capable of accomplishing. However, what you learn only has power when it is put into action.

If just learning new things would help us succeed faster, then all the libraries around the world would be packed. What you learn is important, but what action you take will be what creates the success you desire. Moving what you learn to action is what it is all about.

The two ways you learn are through self-development and experiences in life.

Learning through your self-development

Your self-development is all about the books you read, the audio you listen to, and the educational videos and quality TV programs you watch. Successful people are life-long learners. They know that their self-development is what is going to move them ahead in life and is a critical part of them reaching their goals and the success they desire. It is the same for you.

Your achievements and your ability in getting things done is often directly proportional to how big you grow *you*, and your own self-development plan is a major part of it.

What you learn is not enough. Remember, it is about putting it into action. Here's a tip to use during your self-development: Whenever you do your self-development and read, listen, or watch something interesting, stop and ask the following question: *How can I apply this to my life?*

> Whenever you do your self-development and read, listen, or watch something interesting, stop and ask the following question: *How can I apply this to my life?*

When you hear something interesting and don't think more about it, you file it away into your brain in a *that's interesting* category. This might be some useful information for you, but you didn't think about how you might be able to use it. Why not include one extra step in your self-development?

Ask yourself: How can I apply this to my life? If you answer this question and think about the possible ways you could use what you learned, then what you are doing is moving it from a *that's interesting* category to an action category in your brain.

Your brain will associate what you have learned with the possible ways you would apply it (the actions) and store it that way. You will then see the power behind this in the future. When you encounter an experience that matches what you learned and the way you could apply it, your brain will offer up the possible actions to you—just like magic. Why? Because you have stored what you learned in an *action* way versus just a *that's interesting* way.

Why not try this during your own self-development, and you will store what you learned in your brain in an action way.

Learning through your experiences in life

The second way you learn is from the experiences you have in your life. These come from all the interactions you have during your daily life and from the key relationships you build with others.

You can apply a similar tip as described earlier regarding self-development and ask yourself the following question after key experiences you have each day: *What did I learn from this experience and how can I apply this to my life?*

It is just one question, but it can make the difference between you using what you learned from your daily experiences in the future or not.

Always ask yourself: *How can I apply this to my life?* This question will help you put what you learned into action and will help get things done in the future.

> After key experiences you have each day, ask, What did I learn from this experience and how can I apply this to my life?

Take what you learn and put it into action...

- Through your self development: How can I apply this to my life?
- Through your experiences in life: What did I learn from this experience and how can I apply it to my life?
- You get more done when you apply what you learn.

TRUTH

17

Be more proactive than reactive by thinking ahead

There is an old saying, if you fail to plan, you plan to fail. That is true, and your ability to get things done comes down to whether you take a proactive or reactive approach to life. Everyone achieves more when they take a more proactive approach to life and think ahead to get more accomplished.

For many people, life just seems to keep sneaking up on them. They are going through life reacting to everything that hits them and then wondering why they are not getting anything done that they wanted to do. Because they are just reacting to everyone else, they are just doing what everyone else wants them to do. Does this situation sound familiar to you? Do you feel that you are doing more of what others want than what you really want?

With such a fast pace to life today, you need to think ahead and make sure you schedule your week in a way that you get to achieve what you want to achieve, versus doing only what others want you to achieve. Thinking ahead makes you proactive versus reactive.

Thinking ahead makes you pro-active versus reactive.

This upfront thinking is the time when you remind yourself of what is most important to you and then you refine your focus for the coming week. You could say that your most important thinking activity is to be continually refining your focus. Remember, it is all about focus management, not time management.

The time you invest in both creating and maintaining your focus will pay you 10 times over in productivity to get more done during your week.

Also, your time thinking ahead is when you do your quality thinking on the key outcomes you would like to accomplish. These are the key outcomes that will take you closer to what you want and will drive your actions to accomplish them. You may recall, Noah didn't wait to build the ark until after the rain started. He made a plan ahead of time and then took the action.

Thinking ahead not only helps you to be more productive, but it also enables you to get more help from others. When you think ahead, you usually have more time to arrange the help of others to accomplish more of what you want to achieve. Getting things done is always a factor of what you need to do and about what help you can get from others. The think ahead time helps you create a plan of action

Remember, it is all about focus management, not time management.

that gets the most done by utilizing both yourself and others in the most productive ways possible.

Lastly, thinking ahead enables you to quickly refocus how you use your time when the priorities change. Many people talk about multitasking, but what you are really doing is just one task at a time. What is happening is that rapid refocusing and planning ahead allows you to have thought through everything in advance. This enables you to move quickly from one task to another (rapid refocusing).

Most of the productive people you see are good at rapid refocusing. Their investment in thinking ahead has enabled them to understand well what needs to get done and to know how they will accomplish it, because it has been planned ahead of time. This allows them to refocus themselves from one task to another—and quickly. Why? Because they have already thought through what to do, they don't have to think through what to do each time they change the task. They have to only refocus the mind to the new task, and this gets them quickly into the action.

You can do the same. Invest the time up front to think through the key actions you need to take, and you will become a master at rapid refocusing. The more you master rapid refocusing, the more you will get done every day.

Thinking and planning ahead helps you focus your time to accomplish more.

- Thinking ahead helps you plan better actions.
- Thinking and planning ahead enables you to schedule your time more productively.
- Thinking ahead enables rapid refocusing.

18

Planning drives faster decisions and action

In reality, a plan is outdated the minute it has been completed, because the world is moving so fast these days. However, the very act of creating a plan forces you to think through what you want to accomplish in such detail that it provides you a great understanding to make faster decisions as you take action.

When you plan ahead and think things through in advance, you often think about the possible situations that you might encounter and what the possible implications could be. This leads you to think about your own options in addressing any of the possibilities, and this helps you to be much better prepared. By driving your thinking and planning deeper and broader on the subject, you develop a much better understanding about what you want to accomplish and the different options you have to achieve it.

This understanding is valuable as you go through each day and week. You have to integrate only the newest information to your existing plan, and this enables you to make faster decisions. Your upfront thinking and planning has given you a more complete understanding, and this provides you the confidence to make faster decisions and take quicker action.

> By driving your thinking and planning deeper and broader on the subject, you develop a much better understanding about what you want to accomplish and the different options you have to achieve it.

You often see leaders with the ability to understand complex topics quickly and make those fast decisions. When you see this, you get quite impressed and think they are intelligent, as they are able to understand these complex topics quickly. However, it is often the case that they are no more intelligent than many others. It is just that they invested the time to do their upfront planning and thought everything through on the topics and in some detail ahead of time. This allows them to quickly integrate any new information and respond just as fast. So can you!

Your ability to make decisions faster and with more confidence can become a major factor in getting more done. How many times have you put off deciding something and because you didn't make any decision, you were also not taking any action. You have never seen a successful person who had trouble making decisions. Why? Because successful people know that decisions are what keeps the action going and that delaying decisions means delaying action.

Investing in the upfront planning and thinking is what can enable you to think through the decisions that are coming up in your week and enables you to do some quality thinking and understanding of the key factors and information that will drive those decisions. It is important to set aside the time to invest in the upfront planning and thinking.

The most successful people block off at least 30 minutes each week to think ahead to the possible decisions that they need to make that week. This is the time they actually decide if they need any further information, and if they do, they request it right away. Think back in your own life, and you will think of many times where you were uncomfortable making a fast decision simply because you did not feel you had all the information. This planning and thinking ahead helps you uncover that missing information sooner and allows you to make your decisions faster.

Planning and thinking ahead enables you to make faster decisions.

- Thinking things through in advance helps you to reach conclusions faster.

- Upfront thinking enables you to integrate any new information quickly.

- Thinking ahead means you will always be better prepared than others because you invested time.

TRUTH

19

You can't wait for the inspiration to take action

Do you ever put off the things that you know you should be doing? If you are as others, you probably procrastinate more than you would like. Procrastination is always putting off what you can do today, or what you could do even right now. When you procrastinate on what's most important to you, then what you are doing is pushing your future further into the future.

Successful people are action-oriented and don't wait for the inspiration to take the necessary actions. They have their goals that they want to achieve, and they stay focused on those goals all the time. For these successful people, they know that if they take the necessary actions, the inspiration will then come along to help complete them.

How many times have you put off an important task because you just didn't feel like doing it, or that it was a rather difficult one; and you thought you didn't know where to start it? In fact, you may have even put that task off for days, weeks, or even months.

A great example of this is creating your tax return. You look at it as difficult or time-consuming, and you just don't feel the inspiration to start it. However, after you have started on the work, the inspiration came to finish it, and it actually took a lot less time than you originally thought. So you see, the inspiration came to you to finish it, but only after you took the action to get the task started.

> **Successful people are action-oriented and expect the inspiration will come to finish the task after they start it.**

Successful people are action-oriented and expect the inspiration will come to finish the task after they start it. They *expect* to get the feeling to do it only after they actually start the task. This is the opposite for unsuccessful people. Unsuccessful people have to feel like doing it before taking any action.

You could summarize the difference with the following definitions of both successful people and unsuccessful people:

Successful people let their behaviors drive their feelings.
Unsuccessful people let their feelings drive their behaviors.

Do you see the difference?

Unsuccessful people go through life always waiting for the inspiration and take action only when they feel like it. Successful people are just the opposite. They are constantly taking action and often make many more mistakes than the unsuccessful people ever do. However, the successful people are always moving forward by taking the action, versus the unsuccessful people who are just staying still.

How about another example? Let's take the example of what happens to many salespeople. Salespeople often have to talk to many potential customers until they find one who will buy. Every time a potential customer says no, the salespeople get a negative feeling, and maybe that negative feeling gets even bigger with every no the salesperson receives. Soon, the salesperson starts to delay (procrastinate) calling potential customers and calls fewer potential customers each day. If you were this salesperson, what do you think would happen to the level of sales you would make if you called fewer and fewer people each day? You would get such a negative feeling every time you heard a no that you would call potential customers less and less to avoid the feeling of rejection (the no's). You would be letting your feelings drive your behaviors.

Your life today is the result of the choices and actions that you have taken up to this point. If you procrastinate on those actions that are important to achieve the life you want, then you are pushing the life you want further into the future. Harold Taylor summarized this well, "Procrastination is giving up what you want most for what you want now."

However, you can do what you need to do every day and achieve what you want in your life if you just remind yourself on a daily basis the following:

- Don't wait for the inspiration to take action.

- Let your behaviors drive your feelings.

- If you wait to take action, you will be behind the others who don't wait.

TRUTH

20

What you do today creates your future

Right now, can you take action in the past? No, it is gone forever. Can you take action in the future? Yes, but that means you would be putting off any action until later—procrastinating. The only way to create a different future for yourself is to take action today. Right now.

To accomplish what you want to in your life, it is all about what you do today—and every day from this day forward. John Wooden, the legendary basketball coach said it best, "Make today your masterpiece."

Your actions today create the future you want, and whatever you don't do today is pushing your future into the future. Remember, your past is gone, and it can only be useful for how to do things better, both today and into the future. The future is not here yet and is determined by what you do today, and today is the place for getting things done.

The key is to focus all your energy on what you can accomplish today. You need to think big about what you want to accomplish (the outcomes), but small on the daily actions you need to achieve the outcomes. The most successful people always focus on the actions they can take daily that will move them closer to the goals they want to achieve. Remember, these successful people always have the big dreams, goals, and outcomes in their mind, but they break those down to the necessary actions that will help them achieve it.

> Your actions today create the future you want, and whatever you don't do today, is pushing your future into the future.

What you do every day is based on your habits. In fact, most of what you do each day is driven more by habit than by thought. If what you do today creates your future, and your habits are what are essentially driving your actions each day, then it makes sense that a great place to start in getting more done each day is to start with your habits.

A great question to ask is whether your current daily habits are helping you make the most of each day. If your current daily habits are not helping you, then think about what you need to do differently.

For most people, the missing daily habits and actions are mostly related to discipline, or to be more specific, the lack of discipline. Why not ask yourself: What daily habits are you lacking the discipline for and what will move you closer to your goals?

As with everything else, the key is getting the answers to this question out of you head and down on paper. You would see a difference in what you accomplish each day if you were to

1. Write down a list of daily habits and the discipline you need to put into them.

2. Make the decision to review this list four times a day.

- Breakfast

- Lunch

- Dinner

- Right before going to bed

The act of reviewing this list of habits and discipline will drive you to take action. By reminding yourself at times when you are already doing something (for example, at meal times), there should be no excuse for not doing this review.

Remember, what you accomplish each day is driven by what you put into your focus. The more you remind yourself of your focus (especially those daily habits), the more you will do it.

Action can only happen in the present, and the sum of your today equals your future.

- Focus on getting the most out of each day.

- It is what you do today that creates your future.

- Put those habits in place that help you make the most of each day.

TRUTH

21

Discipline is doing what's necessary, when it is necessary

You can have the best ideas, define the right outcomes, and have your plans all in place. That's great. However, you also need to create in yourself the discipline to do what is necessary, when it is necessary. Everyone is great at being motivated or disciplined to do what he or she likes, but for you to truly get things done, you need to do what's necessary. Thomas Edison said, "The successful person makes a habit of doing what the failing person doesn't like to do."

The speaker Jim Cathcart created a great question: "How would the person I'd like to be, do the things I am about to do?" After one of his speaking events, one of the participants asked Jim if he had any slogan or saying that could be used to motivate him every day. Jim said he didn't have any slogan but offered the participant that question.

> How would the person I'd like to be, do the things I am about to do?

The key is doing what's necessary, but necessary for what? The *what* is the success you defined both for what you want to achieve and for the lifestyle you would like to have. The necessary is what you need to do each day that takes you closer to what you want. Jim Cathcart's question is one of the best ways to both focus you on what's necessary and to motivate you to do it.

The discipline to do what's necessary is powered by the why behind what you want. To become successful and achieve what you want, you will often have to do what's necessary and when it is necessary, and even the tasks you don't like to do. The difference between successful and unsuccessful people is often just that. Successful people are willing to do what unsuccessful people are unwilling to do.

The will to do it is driven by the why. A why has to be powerful enough to provide the will to do what's necessary. If you find yourself not doing what you know you should be doing, then go back and build the why bigger behind what you want.

The why powers you to do the necessary. Build your why big enough so that it will power you to do the necessary, when it is necessary.

If you are like others, you are always putting off those tasks you really should be doing, and they are the very ones that will take you closer to what you want. You could call those tasks your necessary evils. To you, they are evil, as you seem to always be avoiding them. However, these "evils" are the tasks that you absolutely need to do.

One idea is to always focus first on those necessary tasks that you don't like to do. If you build the drive to do those first in your day, the rest of the day becomes much easier, as you then begin to do all the other tasks you enjoy doing. Just by doing all those necessary evils first, you will accomplish more every day.

Why not make a list of those necessary tasks and put the list in a place where it will remind you daily.

Focus on doing the "necessary" first each day. The discipline to do the necessary is the foundation for success.

- It's either the pain of discipline or the pain of regret.

- The why creates the power and discipline to do the necessary.

- You have never seen an undisciplined successful person.

TRUTH

You create your habits and your habits create you

What you do daily and what you accomplish is based a great deal on your habits. They often say that you can tell how successful a person will be just by looking at their habits. If this is the case, then it is true that you create your habits and your habits create you.

People are doing this all the time. They keep doing the same things (the habits) but expect different results. You can never accomplish anything great in your life without changing your habits first.

Experts say that it takes at least 28 days to establish a new habit. By establishing a habit, this means to repeat if often enough that you have taken what was uncomfortable to you and have made it comfortable.

You cannot really change your life, and get more of the *right* things done, unless you change your habits. If every day you do the same things, then you have to expect the same results. Albert Einstein defined this as, "Insanity: doing the same thing over and over again and expecting different results."

> You cannot really change your life, and get more of the *right* things done, unless you change your habits.

If you want different results, then you need to decide what habits you need to create. If you make the commitment to change your habits and stick with it for at least 28 days, then you have the way to create different results.

Here's a great example of making something a habit from comedian Jerry Seinfeld. Jerry knew that success for him was in writing better jokes and the way to create better jokes was to write every day. He had a technique he used, and you can use it to motivate yourself—even when you don't feel like it. His technique involved a unique calendar system he used to drive himself to write. Here's how it works.

Jerry had a calendar that had a whole year on one page and a red marker. Each day that he wrote, he marked an X on that calendar day. Jerry explained, "After a few days you'll have a chain. Just keep at it and the chain will grow longer every day. You'll like seeing that chain, especially when you get a few weeks under your belt. Your only job next is to not break the chain. Don't break the chain."

Why not begin a chain for the key habit that would make the most difference in your life. In fact, most people are only one or two key habits away from becoming successful in their chosen career. However, these habits are more often related to a person's character than to any other abilities that they might have. If you were to study the core character traits of successful people, you would notice two key character traits that all of them possess. They are *discipline* and *commitment.*

All successful people have made the commitment to themselves to take whatever action is necessary for them to achieve their goals. Their commitment is visible to others by the discipline they have and by the habits they have put into their daily lives to guarantee that those actions taken.

You can see that the habits are what are making these successful people so successful. They have created the habits, and their habits have created their success.

You can do the same. If you create the *right* habits, your habits will create you and the success you desire.

Focus on your habits and your habits will enable your success.

- Your habits are the foundation for your actions.

- Your daily actions are what creates the success you desire.

- You create your habits and then your habits create you.

TRUTH

23

That little bit extra makes a huge difference

Look at the sports world and the famous 100M races at the Olympics. The difference between the winner and second place is often just a couple hundreds of a second. The winner was only just a little bit faster, but it made a huge difference in the result, as usually nobody remembers who came in second.

What do you think contributed to that little difference in time but a big difference in result? Often, it has come down to that little bit extra the winner did in preparation for the race. Maybe an extra 15 minutes stretching every day, skipping those unhealthy foods that he or she loved, or maybe even some small differences in the preparation done the day before the race.

Many people think there is always a big difference between first and second place—both in sports and in life. However, it is almost always that little bit extra that creates the big difference. The difference between first and second is often just that little bit extra of discipline that's inside one person and not the other.

> The difference between first and second is often just that little bit extra of discipline that's inside one person and not the other.

Think about your own life and how you prepare for meetings at your job. Many times the difference between a successful and unsuccessful meeting is whether the preparation was done. That preparation is usually not taking much time, but if you didn't discipline yourself to do it, it wouldn't get done. This little extra of preparation can make all the difference between a successful meeting and an unsuccessful one.

How about another example? Salespeople understand that the more they know about a customer, the better the questions they can ask in uncovering the true customer's needs, and whether their products and services can help the customer. However, most salespeople do not always do their preparation, and it often is just a little extra investment of time to look up on the Internet some information about the customer and the company they will be visiting.

If you were to think about similar situations in your own life, you would certainly be able to think of countless situations where that little bit extra could have made a big difference for you. The key is to develop the discipline to always give that little bit extra. If you do, you will differentiate yourself from those who won't.

It is difficult to do that little extra and set yourself apart from the others if you are constantly staying with the crowd.

There's a basic concept that highlights this point. If you do what everyone else is doing, by default, you are just one of the crowd. It is difficult to do that little extra and set yourself apart from the others if you are constantly staying with the crowd. Why not separate yourself from the crowd?

Setting a goal of giving a little bit extra every day could have a tremendous impact on your life and the success you will achieve. That little bit extra is almost never in the difficult tasks but in the easy tasks that are often difficult to do.

Give that little bit extra that others are not willing to give.

- A little extra every day can make the difference.
- Strive to do what others are unwilling to do.
- Make it a habit of going that extra bit.

TRUTH

People really don't fail, they just stop taking action

If you talk to successful entrepreneurs, they can always tell you about the critical time when things were going bad and everyone else thought that they should quit. Well, they didn't quit and kept taking action, as they had the belief that if they just keep at it long enough they would be successful.

A great example of this is the life of President Lincoln. He is remembered for his leadership during one of the most difficult times in U.S. history. President Lincoln experienced many setbacks in his life—more than most of us would experience in multiple lifetimes. He failed in two businesses, lost over seven elections, and experienced a total nervous breakdown. Yet, he went on to become the president of the United States because he kept taking action. He never quit.

Many people stop just short of success because they just quit.

Many people stop just short of success because they just quit. If you read the biographies of successful entrepreneurs, you will find that many times they could have easily failed if they stopped taking action. Many of them faced at least one challenge in their lives when it looked as if nothing could be done to overcome it. However, they didn't quit and kept taking action until they worked their way through the challenges.

Everyone encounters challenges they must overcome in their lives. These challenges are the ones that help you to grow stronger. The difference is that successful people have the perseverance to keep taking action, no matter what type of challenge they face. They have the belief inside them that they will be able to meet any challenge or solve any problem that comes their way.

Look again at the example of President Lincoln. He could have quit running for office and just given up on life with all the troubles he encountered. You see many people giving up on life today, and they have faced only a fraction of the challenges that President Lincoln faced. However, he kept strong in what he wanted to contribute in his life and just kept taking action.

The people who achieve success in their lives have perseverance.

You become a failure only when you stop taking action. The people who achieve success in their lives have perseverance. They will stick with what's important to them because they have the belief in themselves that they will ultimately accomplish it.

Everyone has problems in their lives, and the bigger the goals you would like to accomplish, the bigger the problems that will be there for you to solve. There are many people who think the opposite and that the more success they achieve, the easier the problems they will encounter. You will always have problems or challenges in your life in equal proportion to the goals you set for yourself.

The difference between the successful and the unsuccessful people is all about how they view the problems and their approach to them. Robert Schuller said it best, "Problems are not stop signs; they are guidelines." The people who look at problems as stop signs are always giving up too soon, and often at the step where their success would be just starting for them, if only they kept at it.

People who don't quit have perseverance. Perseverance comes from the belief that they will do it. So can you.

- You only fail when you stop taking action.

- Success comes when you don't give up when others will.

- Action is the way to face any challenge or problem.

TRUTH

25

It is easier to create a new habit than break an old one

If you are like others, you have habits that you wished you didn't have. You have probably also tried to break the habit several times with no success. To break a habit, you have to continually think about not doing it and instead always think about the thing you would like to stop. Does that sound like a great way for you to break a habit, by having to constantly think about what you don't want to do?

It is often that several of your old habits are what are preventing you from becoming better at getting things done. A far easier approach is to create a new habit that could replace the old one. If you just focused on the creation of the new habit, you would be focusing your mind on something positive and creating something new—versus focusing on something negative.

Many examples of this can be seen in daily life. For example, many people want to stop smoking. Smoking has an addictive component, but often the problem is that people need to continually remind themselves to not smoke.

People who replace old habits with new ones are far more successful at having these new habits stick.

Many people who have successfully quit have replaced the smoking habit with something else. Some, when they felt the urge for a smoke, just went on a short walk.

The same is true for people who want to lose weight. The people who are always focused on what they shouldn't eat are never really successful at staying on their diet and losing the weight they want. It is always the people who have decided on a completely different diet that have put their total focus on eating something new, versus trying to stop eating as much of something they are used to and like. The important point is that people who replace old habits with new ones are far more successful at having these new habits stick.

These examples are large ones; however, there are many small habits that you do, day in and day out, which are not helping you to get what you want.

Always ask yourself the following question about the habits you currently have. Do my habits help me to get closer to what I want to achieve and the life I want to live? Ask this question for each habit, and if the habit is not helping you to get closer to what you want, then it is a target to be replaced.

Do my habits help me to get closer to what I want to achieve and the life I want to live?

Next, for all the habits that are not taking you closer to what you want to achieve in your life, think about the *right* habits you could put in the bad habits place. Remember, everything in your life first begins in your thoughts. This investment of time in thinking through your habits could lead you to put into your life those one or two new habits that will drive your future success.

To break an old habit, focus on creating a new one instead and replace that old one. It is much easier to replace a habit then to just stop an old habit.

- Always think about replacing an old/bad habit with a new one.

- Focusing on the *new* is always a better approach than focusing on stopping the *old*.

- Replacing is always easier than thinking about stopping.

TRUTH

26

You achieve better rapport
by adapting your approach
to others

Your life is all about relationships, both the professional and personal ones. The more you create rapport with others, the more you feel you trust them and they trust you. If you think about it, do you act exactly the same way when you are with all your friends? Maybe not, and you might have learned about how to create better rapport with new people you meet—both the professional and personal ones.

You know the golden rule says, "Do unto others as you would have them do unto you." Well, Dr. Tony Alessandra developed the platinum rule, which is, "Do unto others as they would like to be done unto." Tony has highlighted the key to building better rapport with others. People don't want to be treated the way you would like to be treated. They want to be treated the way they like to be treated.

It is far too often that people expect others to like what they like and react to the world in the same way. However, it just doesn't work that way. Everyone has different personalities and has grown up with different experiences, and to be successful in your communications, you need to both understand this and adapt your approach.

> It is far too often that people expect others to like what they like and react to the world in the very same way.

There's a great story to look at this by using the analogy of a hamburger. There are some people who are tremendously focused and don't want any small talk (the bun) with their conversations with others. They want only the facts (the meat) and usually keep any small talk to an absolute minimum.

However, there are others who won't listen to the facts (the meat), without first engaging in small talk. They would feel uncomfortable if someone started the conversation right away with the facts (the meat) and didn't engage in any small talk at all.

You need to construct the hamburger of conversations in a different way for everyone you meet. By adapting your approach to the other person's preferred style of communicating, you will create greater rapport. When you create greater rapport, you will get the other person to listen more closely to what you are saying. Communication is never an outcome. It is only an activity. It is all about having the other person understanding you and doing what you want. That is the desired outcome.

When you create greater rapport, you will get the other person to listen more closely to what you are saying.

How about an example? Many bosses experience this problem with some of their people. Bosses tend to be extremely driven and focused on getting things done. Also, they are usually busy, and in all their conversations, they tend to get right to the point and begin right with (the meat). However, they always have some employees in their organization who get nervous when speaking to their boss and often are not listening closely at the beginning of any conversation with their boss. If the boss gets right to (the meat) with this type of person, there's a good chance that their people are not listening clearly in the beginning of the conversation. The better approach for the boss would be to engage in some small talk to put the other person at ease before talking about the details (the meat).

The same problem often happens in reverse. The employee comes into the boss talking about the weather, and so on—lots of small talk (the bun)—and the boss becomes more frustrated every second this continues. The boss wants to get right down to business (the meat) and finds all that small talk a waste of time.

In both these situations between the boss and the employee, they would have much better interactions if each were trying to adapt to the other. So can you. The more you adapt to others, the more they will adapt to you. Adapt your approach to others for greater success.

- Treat people as they would like to be treated.
- Adapt your approach to build greater rapport.
- Before every conversation, think about how you need to construct the hamburger.

TRUTH

27

Remove the emotions first, and then discuss the facts

In your life you will always encounter people who get emotional over an issue, and you either deal with it or run from it. Of course, the best approach is to deal with it, but in the right way. People who get emotional will want to express it, and not listen to your logic or the facts, and understanding this can make a bigger difference.

People who get emotional will always want the opportunity to share what they are feeling first before engaging in other discussions. It is important for you to acknowledge what they are feeling and their concerns and to be a good listener to what they have to say. In many ways, it is all about the follow-up questions you ask that make others feel that you are both interested and listening and that you want to understand what they are feeling.

Too many people try to use logic and the facts to argue a point with someone who is already emotional. This never works, as the emotional person is not in the mood to listen and is just in the mood to share what they are feeling. During these times, there is no use in trying to share any more information, as it will never help the situation and probably only make it worse.

The goal here is to remove the emotions first.

This is the time to simply listen and to ask questions that will allow the other person to share completely their thoughts and what they are feeling. Until the other person has shared their feelings to a level that makes them feel more at ease or comfortable, you should never try to share any more information from your side.

The goal here is to remove the emotions first. Once you have allowed the other person to share completely their thoughts and emotions, then and only then can you begin by sharing your information and the facts behind the issue. The listening of the other person's feelings will "earn" you the right with them to then share your information.

Unfortunately, this is not always the way people treat these situations. How many times have you become emotional on an issue and the other person was just trying to convince you with all the facts and information they knew why they were right. I would guess that after the first few facts you stopped listening and this only increased the level of emotions on both sides of the issue.

Also, you might have experienced the opposite when you were dealing with an issue and the other person was getting emotional. You might have thought that it is best to stick to the facts and the information and take the emotion out of the argument. The more you shared the facts, information, and logic behind the issue, the more emotional the other person became. What happened is that you didn't allow the other person to share their feelings before you shared your information.

As you can see with these examples, you always need to remove the emotions first and then discuss the facts. The main reason why people don't do this is the lack of time and patience. Most people feel that they don't have the time to just listen to others thoughts and feelings, and their lack of patience drives them to force the issue quicker and with more facts and information.

To become more effective in dealing with emotional situations and difficult issues, always be patient and invest the time to listen to the other person's thoughts and feelings. Almost always, once you have listened, you will then "earn" the right, from the other person, to share your side (the facts).

> Others will not listen to you until they have been able to share how they are feeling.

Remember to remove the emotions first and then discuss the facts. Others will not listen to you until they have been able to share how they are feeling.

- Be prepared to listen before sharing what you want them to know.

- Listening and empathizing first earns you the right to share your information.

- Have the patience to LISTEN.

TRUTH

28

You are in "sales," as you are always selling your ideas to others

Talk to anyone about salespeople, and you will either get a positive or negative reaction. Nobody ever seems to be neutral on the topic of salespeople. However, you and others should be positive about sales, as you are all in sales. You might not be in the selling profession, but you are in the profession of selling yourself and your ideas.

Everyone is in sales, as everyone needs to sell themselves to others. How you communicate and package your key messages can make a big difference in what you are able to achieve and the help you can get from others. You are selling your ideas and the value you can bring to others around you. The more value they see in working with you, the more help you will get from them in achieving what you want.

People need to buy into your ideas before they buy into you.

Too many people think first about what others need to understand from them. They are constantly focusing on the information they need to share and end up sharing far too much information, and this results in boring people. To be more effective in selling your ideas to others, it is better to focus first on being more persuasive than informative.

Selling is all about buying and getting others to understand your ideas and the value you can bring to them. To understand selling, you need to understand buying as you need to first get others to buy into what you are saying. People need to buy into your ideas before they buy into you.

As with sales, the most important thing is to focus your communications on the other person. What is the other person interested in and what do they want to hear? Also, think about what you want the other person to understand and feel about what you want to say.

The focus of all good communications is first focused on who you are communicating to and second on what you want to communicate. By focusing on whom you are communicating to, you think ahead on what you will say and how it will be interpreted, and this enables you to tailor your communications to meet their expectations.

Selling your ideas and selling yourself is never about having the focus on you. It is all about placing the focus on the other person and how you can help him or her with what they want. By helping others get what they want, you will always get their attention and bring the focus back to you in return.

Think about what you want the other person to understand and feel about what you want to say.

Remember, you are always selling your ideas to others, and this is what enables you to get help in achieving what you want in life.

- To understand selling you need to understand buying. It is how others will receive what you say.

- The ability to influence others (selling) is a fundamental skill for success.

- You are in sales because you must always be selling your ideas to others.

TRUTH

29

Questions have more power
than answers

If two people are having a conversation together, one is asking all the questions and one is providing all the answers. Which person is in control of the conversation? It's the questions that have more power than answers, as the questions control the conversation.

Questions help you to control the conversations with other people, and this helps you to focus those conversations more on what helps you to get what you want. If you are not asking the questions in your conversations with others, then others are controlling the conversations and focusing the discussions on what they want versus what you want.

Questions show that you are interested in what others have to say. By showing interest in others, others will show interest in you.

Questions are also powerful in building relationships. Questions show that you are interested in what others have to say. By showing interest in others, others will show interest in you. Also, questions have the power to influence others. How? Because questions help others to think and think about something they never realized before. You gain more influence with others by asking them questions that make them think than you do by just providing them any answers.

Questions are the fuel that enables you to tailor communication and key messages to others. You always have more effective conversations when you get others talking first. They share their thoughts with you and information that will enable you to "package" your thoughts and ideas back to them by using their words and not yours.

Everyone shares their ideas and explains things in different ways and with different words. By asking questions up front to uncover these differences, it then allows you to match others ways and words in sharing your own ideas back to them. This helps you to get your ideas understood faster by others.

If you are a leader, questions are what help your people to think through the solutions, versus just you providing them the answers.

Every time you provide answers to your people, you are taking back a little bit of the ownership of the solution, as they will be executing your solution based on your answers, and not theirs.

Questions have the power to help people see the answers on their own and, thus, keep the ownership of executing the solution driven by their answers, not yours. You could say that questions are like an investment of time for leaders, as they get their people thinking and developing the answers on their own. However, providing answers is just the opposite, and is like spending time, as you have saved your people from thinking (and growing).

You can also see the power of questions in sales. The old saying goes, "If the customer is talking, you are winning. If you are talking, you are losing." Questions get others talking and sharing more of their ideas and information with you. When you understand others better, you have the "fuel" to influence others better. Questions show interest and interest drives influence.

Why not do a mini-review after all the conversations you have this week. Ask yourself, "How were my questions to answers ratio?" Could you phrase the question, "How was my listen versus talk ratio?"

In all your interactions and conversations with others, questions have more power than answers.

Questions put you in control of conversations.

- Questions have the power to influence others. It gets them THINKING!

- Questions show your interest in others.

- Questions keep others with the ownership.

TRUTH

30

Stories and examples make the emotional link faster

If you look at the best speakers, they are usually also the best storytellers. Great speakers are telling stories, providing examples, and linking any information in their speeches to these stories and examples. They know that stories and examples get people more involved in the talk, as everyone is paying attention and trying to follow the story or example.

To get the help of others, you often need to grab their attention and get them to listen to you closely, and to what you have to say. More than any other communication idea, the use of stories and examples will make the emotional link with others faster and get them interested in what you have to say. When you have their interest, they will listen to you more closely.

You always get your ideas received by others much faster and easier if you tell them a story or example of how it can be true first. If you skipped the stories or examples and just told them only the information behind the ideas you are sharing, others might be suspicious if it were actually true. However, by telling the stories or examples, others see how this could be true and accept the information and the ideas you then share with them.

Once you have reached people emotionally, they are then listening to you in a much more interested way and will listen more closely to the information you provide.

People buy emotionally and justify what they want to buy intellectually. It is the same when they are listening to others. They will listen to others more closely if they are emotionally engaged in what is being said than just intellectually engaged. Stories and examples provide the ability to reach people more on an emotional level. Once you have reached them emotionally, they are then listening to you in a much more interested way and will listen more closely to the information you provide.

Stories and examples are also important for leaders. Just like speakers, leaders need to communicate new ideas and information

118

to their people and get them motivated to take action on these new ideas and information. The best leaders do the same as the best speakers. They are constantly using stories and examples in their communications with their people.

The best leaders are often using stories and examples in the place of answers to their people. Instead of just providing their people the answers to their questions or problems, the best leaders tell their people a story or example that helps them answer their own question or solve their own problem.

So, you can see that stories and examples are the best way for others to learn. Others learn more from applying what they learn from the stories and examples than they do from just the basic information they hear.

You can see the power in using stories and examples. When sharing any new information with others, always begin by telling a story or an example that either uses the information in it or shows how this information could be true, as the story or example provides the proof.

To become a better communicator and influencer of others, become a better storyteller. When you spark people's interest in the story or the example, you have them listening more closely to what you have to say. When they are listening closely to you, you then have the ability to influence them. Attach any new concepts or ideas to stories and examples of how it could be true.

- Stories and examples make the emotional link with others.

- With stories and examples, people can see how it can be true.

- Stories and examples always keep the listener's attention.

TRUTH

31

Match communication styles for a quicker responses

Communication capabilities and methods have increased over the years, and today there are so many ways to communicate (email, phone, texting, and so on—and as always in person), and not everyone has the same preference when it comes to the way they like to communicate. How you match others preferences can make a big difference in the effectiveness of your communications.

Think about it. You have your own preference on the way you like to both send and receive any communications from others. You will naturally use your preferred way more than others, and if people were to take notice of how you communicate, they would see that as well.

You are more productive if others use your preferred way of communicating. If you prefer email, you will be more productive if others use email when communicating

> You are more productive if others use your preferred way of communicating.

to you. However, if you were the opposite and hated email, would you want others to email you? Probably not. Everyone has his or her preferred way of communicating.

If you are more productive with one way over another, you should tell others your preferred way. If they use your preferred way, you will be more productive. If you like email, wouldn't you be more productive if others used emails to communicate with you?

However, to get things done, it is not always about others communicating to you, but also you communicating to others. In this case, it is more effective for you to match the preferred way of others when communicating with them.

You have probably experienced this for yourself. You often try to call another person on the phone and seem to never be able to reach him or her. However, if you send an email, the same person is right back to you from their Blackberry in five minutes. Clearly, the preferred way of communicating for this person was email.

Alternatively, you also know people who hate email. Every time you send an email, you never get a response. However, when you call him or her, you seem to always reach them right away. Again, the preferred way of this person is probably not email but phone.

It is important to keep in mind that communication is just an activity. The real outcome of the communication is others doing what you would like them to do. By using other's preferred way of communicating, you are probably getting them to act on your communication much faster than if you used a way of communicating they didn't necessarily like. Matching other's preferred ways of communicating will get them to take action on what you want faster.

Also, if others use your preferred way of communicating, you will be far more productive. So, for others that need to regularly communicate with you, tell them your preferred way of communicating. The more they use your preferred way, the more productive you are. For example, if you like to communicate via email, and more people use email with you, you will be more productive in your communications.

Focus on matching others ways of communicating, and you will often get faster responses to your communications. And, isn't this what communicating is all about: others responding and acting on your communications. Tell others your preferred communication method to be more productive, and to get better action from others, use their preferred method.

> **Focus on matching others ways of communicating, and you will often get faster responses to your communications.**

- Others using your preferred way of communicating makes you more productive.

- Using other's preferred way of communicating always gets a faster response.

- Matching ways of communicating can save you time.

TRUTH

32

Listening enables better communication more than talking

If you want to build relationships faster, you do it by learning more about others than others learning more about you. The old saying captures this best: "How do I know how much I care about you until I know how much you care about me." Listening is what enables you to learn more about others and enables better communication than talking.

Listening shows that you are interested in what others have to say. When you show interest, other people will then feel more important, and making other people feel important is the fastest way to build relationships and for others to be willing to help you in the future.

Most people's favorite topic is themselves, and this is why everyone likes to talk about him or herself. However, doing all the talking is only proving to others that you feel you are more important than they are. Why not be different and strive to do more listening than talking?

You find it in many conversations where people don't like to listen in the conversations they have. What they are really doing throughout the conversation is thinking of what they want to say next when the opportunity comes for them to talk.

> The more you listen to others and ask follow-up questions, the more you will be able to influence them.

You cannot give others your full attention and truly listen to them if you are thinking of what you want to say next all the time.

Listening becomes powerful for you when you listen attentively and then ask follow-up questions that will get others to share even more about what they were talking about. Successful salespeople use the power of the follow-up question all the time. The more the sales person understands the customer's business and specific needs, the better he or she can deliver services to meet those needs. The same goes for you. The more you listen to others and ask follow-up questions, the more you will be able to influence them.

Here's an interesting question. Two people are having a conversation together. One person is asking all the questions, and the other person is providing all the answers. Which person is in control of the conversation? The person asking the questions, right?

This is the first benefit of listening. When you are asking the questions and listening, you are in control of the conversations with others. If you are in control of the conversation, you are more likely to reach the result of the conversation you would like.

The second benefit of listening is what you will learn. You cannot learn more from your conversations

When you are asking the questions and listening, you are in control of the conversations with others.

if you are doing all the talking. When you are asking questions and listening, you get to learn more from others and this is helping you to grow faster. No one can grow fast enough on just their own experiences, and by listening to others, you are able to use what you learned from their experiences and apply them to your own life.

The third benefit of listening is in the power of building relationships. You always create a better rapport and understand better how to approach others when you do more listening than talking. Also, nothing builds stronger relationships than making a note of the important things others say and then remembering them sometime into the future when seeing them again. The proof of listening is in the remembering, and it is the remembering that makes others feel important. When you make others feel important, you build stronger relationships.

To get more done in your life, you need to surround yourself with people who are willing to help you get what you want and for you to help others to get what they want. Listening is the fuel that builds those key relationships.

Listening helps you to build stronger relationships with others.

- Listen to understand, not to speak next.

- Your remembering is the proof to others of your listening.

- Listening is the fuel for building relationships with others.

TRUTH

33

No one creates success by themselves

Whatever you want to accomplish in your life, you will never be able to achieve it all on your own. No one really creates success by themselves, and in many ways, the level of success you will achieve is linked to how well you can work with others and get their help.

You can never accomplish everything you would like to on your own, so you need to be able to work with others to accomplish what you want and achieve that success you desire. How effectively you get along with others can be a major factor in achieving that success. Your people skills are what will help you more than any other skill to get the *right* help from others.

Everyone is different, and your ability to adapt to these differences will help you to get more help and achieve more in return. It is far too often that projects often fail because two people with different personalities just couldn't get along. Focus your energy on what you want to achieve and not on what you wanted to do differently than others are suggesting or doing.

> You can never accomplish everything you would like to on your own, so you need to be able to work with others to accomplish what you want and achieve that success you desire.

Far too often there are people with all the abilities to achieve the success they desire, but they find it difficult to work with others and get their help to achieve it. These types of people are always struggling to work with others who don't do things in the same way. They feel uncomfortable working with others who take a different approach to the tasks to be done and are constantly trying to get others to do it their way. However, everyone is different, and they will never find others doing it exactly their way.

The people who are successful working with others and getting the help of others focus on something completely different. They are not so concerned with how it gets done, but that everyone is focused on the outcome that needs to be achieved. The successful people focus others on the outcomes that need to be achieved and let others determine their own way to get the task done to achieve the outcomes.

You could say that successful people look for others who can help them achieve the *what* (the outcome) and leave it to others to determine their own *how* (the tasks) to achieve it. Successful people know how to adapt to others versus forcing others to adapt to them. The important thing for them is not necessarily getting things done their way but the successful way.

You could say that your ultimate success comes through adapting yourself and serving others. Zig Ziglar says, "You can get everything you want in life by just helping others get what they want." Life works when you give of yourself and that gift always gets returned to you in the form of help from others. By helping others, they will help you in return.

If you are a leader, by helping your people grow, they help you deliver the team's or organization's performance, and this helps you achieve your targets as well. All successful leaders understand this and focus their energy on growing their people. By growing their people, they grow their organization. If the organization grows, it can deliver better performance, and then everything is reflected back on the performance of the leader who inspired the growth and performance of the organization.

One of the traits of successful people is their willingness to teach others. By helping others to learn and grow, they will, in return, get the help from others as well.

Remember, no one achieves success by themselves, and the help you get from others is always a result of how you adapt to and help others first. Success is often based on how well you interact with others.

- Understand that you cannot create success on your own.

- Your ability to adapt to others determines the help you will get from others.

- The more you help others to grow, the more help they give you in return.

TRUTH

34

You attract help from others
by keeping your
commitments

You might have heard the saying, "God helps those who help themselves." You could paraphrase that by saying, "You get help from others when you keep your commitment first." Why? Because when you keep your commitments, others see helping you as a good investment of their time. When you get help from others, you are able to get more accomplished, and you often improve yourself by learning new things.

You see, how you act tells others how to interact with you. If you do not do what you said you would do, then others will prefer not to work with you. Nobody achieves success on his or her own, and you will always need the help of others. Why not be the best by honoring your commitments, and in this way you will attract the help from others.

> When you keep your commitments, others see helping you as a good investment of their time.

Many people do not realize the power that comes from keeping their commitments. In fact, most people go through life not understanding that they have the power within themselves to influence how people will interact with them. Those who understand this know that influence and the ability to get help from others starts by always keeping their commitments.

For example, you have a problem at work and need the help from someone else to solve it. There are two people in the office that could help you. One is focused in his work and always keeping his commitments. The other struggles to keep focused at work and often doesn't deliver on her commitments. Which person would you go ask for help? Most likely you would ask for help from the person who keeps his commitments.

So, this actually works in the opposite way, as well. Just as you would go to the people who keep their commitments for help, they would, in turn, be the first to help you, if you keep your commitments, too. People who keep their commitments attract others who need help, but also in return, they attract others to help them.

It all comes back to the universal principle of "The more you give, the more you get." However, it is also in this case, "The more you have commitment, the more commitment you get from others." You also get the help to achieve what you want to achieve in *your* life.

People will always take the time to help others who have the commitment within them. It is strange that the very people who need the help the most don't often get it. Just as you read in the example, people really don't want to either ask for help or to help people who don't keep their commitments. Why? Because people who don't keep commitments cannot be trusted as much as others, and this is why these people are generally avoided.

You have realized the importance of keeping your commitments. When you focus yourself on keeping your commitments, you will probably end up making fewer commitments than before. If you are like others, you have been making commitments that were more "I'll try" than "It will definitely happen."

When you focus on keeping your commitments, you also get another benefit in return. You get the increase in your own self-esteem and respect for yourself, as you have not only kept your commitments with others, but you are also keeping your commitments with yourself.

When you begin to keep the commitments to yourself, it then becomes much easier to keep the commitments to others. Start today and focus on keeping your commitments and attracting the help from others in getting things done. The way you act is either attracting people to help you or sending them away.

> When you focus yourself on keeping your commitments, you will probably end up making fewer commitments than before.

- If you keep your commitments, others will keep their commitments to you.

- People will always help others who help themselves first.

- Keeping commitments to yourself helps you keep commitments to others.

TRUTH

35

Trust is the fuel for productive teamwork

Nobody creates success on his or her own. To get things done, you will always be a part of teams, and trust is the fuel that creates productive teamwork. Teamwork is getting everyone to work together to achieve a common outcome, and people who trust each other will work more productively with each other to achieve it.

You build trust by getting to know others and learning more about both their professional and personal lives. It is often what you learn about other people's personal lives that provide you with more insight into how they think and feel, as well as what is most important to them. When you know people better, you will understand better their behaviors and then know how best to interact with them to create better teamwork.

The key to building trust is to be comfortable enough to share with others your opinions, even when your opinions will differ from theirs. You know that you have high trust in your team when everyone is willing to open up and share his or her ideas and opinions.

> **The key to building trust is to be comfortable enough to share with others your opinions, even when your opinions will differ from theirs.**

To build trust and maintain it, you always need to allow for the differences in others. The best teams do not have members who are all the same types of person. The differences in the team can be a real strength and can help the team to develop more creative solutions. However, to make it work and to get the benefits, everyone needs to adapt a little to allow for the differences of others. Your ability to adapt your approaches to others can be one of the most important abilities for you in getting things done by others. In fact, one of the key skills of successful leaders is their ability to adapt.

Conflict is something that many people want to avoid, especially in a team environment. However, conflict, if constructive around the issues, is something that makes for much stronger teams. Teams with high trust experience much greater conflict than teams with little trust. Teams with little trust often don't have any conflict, as everyone is afraid to bring up anything that others might disagree with. If your team has little or no conflict, you don't have a high-performing team, as people are not willing to share what they are thinking.

A key skill of successful leaders is their ability to adapt.

You will often need to work in teams to get things done, and they will help you achieve what you want to achieve. To make this happen, you always need to be a "participating" team member and help the team drive toward the outcomes that will create both yours and the team's success. You see so many people who don't "participate" in the teams to which they belong. These people usually attend all the meetings but never really speak. They are not offering their ideas and never contribute to the team, apart from their required work outside the meetings.

Set yourself the goal to always be a participating team member. When you participate, you are "voicing your say" on the direction and the focus of the team. By "participating" you have a greater opportunity to make sure that you can achieve success for both you and the team.

To build trust and get help of others, create an environment where everyone is participating and willing to share what is on their mind. If you build this environment, your team meetings will never be boring, and you will put "everything" on the table to be discussed, versus discussed in personal conversations in the hallway.

Set your goal to *build trust* in whatever teams you belong. Trust drives teamwork. Focus on developing trust with your fellow team members.

- Trust enables people to share what they are thinking.
- The best solutions and outcomes are a result of every team member participating.
- If your team meetings are boring, then you have low trust in your team.

You get the behaviors that you reinforce

Let's say that you have to complete four different tasks for four different people by tomorrow. Three never follow up with you, but the fourth calls you this morning and asks if you will complete it by tomorrow and if you need any help. Which task would you do first? Right, the one for the person who follows up, as her follow-up gets you doing her task first.

There will always be situations where you need something from others by a certain date to keep your commitment to another. How you reinforce (follow-up) the *right* behaviors of others to keep their commitment not only helps them deliver on time in this situation, but in all future situations.

> How you reinforce (follow-up) the *right* behaviors of others to keep their commitment helps them deliver on time.

Take this situation and the example where you need the work from the other person by Wednesday for you to meet the commitment of what you need to provide by Friday. If you politely follow up with the other person on Tuesday and ask if he can complete his work by the next day, then you have much more confidence that his work will be done on time. Also, you have to set the image in the other person's mind that this is important, and he will then probably give it higher priority in his mind as well. You have reinforced the right behaviors because you followed up.

Take this same situation with a slightly different example. You have the same commitments, her work needs to be done by Wednesday, and your work and commitment to others is by Friday. However, this time you do not follow-up on Tuesday and do not follow-up until Friday morning, the day your commitment is due. By following up so late, you are now putting pressure on the other person to deliver quickly so that you can keep your commitment. Do you think she will appreciate that extra pressure? Do you appreciate the extra pressure you have just put on yourself by not following up sooner? Probably not.

There's also another aspect in this second example. Because you didn't follow-up until two days after the day you told the other person you needed the work by, she now thinks that your actual requested dates are not the true requested dates. The next time you need work done from her and request a date, she will think that she actually has a couple extra days to complete it and will probably not put the same priority on meeting your requested date.

You can see that the way you follow-up, or that lack of follow-up, has an impact on the behaviors of others. The examples show that you get the behaviors you reinforce.

These situations and examples are about just following up. However, the way your reinforce other's behaviors can make a difference in many other situations.

For leaders and even parents, how they reinforce the behaviors in their employees and in their children is establishing their behaviors, both today and into the future. For you, just as leaders and parents, how you reinforce the behaviors of others establishes how they will interact with you, both today and into the future.

The best approach is to establish boundaries up front as to what you will consider both good and bad behaviour. When it is discussed up front, there are far less misunderstandings. Then, it is all about how you reinforce those behaviors.

- For good behaviors, thank others for what they did. Give them praise.
- For bad behaviors (outside the boundaries), remind them of what they did and why it is a problem, both for you and for them.

You can see that what you can do to help others deliver on their commitments to you is the same as what leaders and parents need to do as well. You get the behaviors you reinforce (either with your actions or inaction).

- Reinforce both the good and bad behavior of others.
- Always follow up, especially when your credibility is on the line.
- Follow-up equals important and not following up equals the not important.

TRUTH

37

You can't see the picture when you are in the frame

To become better at getting things done, you have to get better yourself. You cannot always see what those improvements need to be, and it is often the feedback that you receive from others that enables you to focus on the right things to improve. It is true. You can't see the picture when you are in the frame.

You always need the feedback from others to help you see those areas in your life where you could improve. In business, you often have those 360-degrees of feedback where you get feedback from people all around you—your peers, bosses, and employees. This feedback gives you some ideas on the areas in your life where your behaviors could be improved.

Everyone has blind spots in their behaviors that they do not see for themselves. If you go through life not getting any feedback from others, then these blind spots stay

> Everyone has blind spots in their behaviors that they do not see for themselves.

invisible to you forever, and you have no way to eliminate them. You cannot improve an area or behaviors in your life that you are not aware of.

To understand these blind spots, you just cannot count on others to always point them out to you. Your family and friends, who are close to you, are often hesitant to talk to you about any of your bad areas or bad behaviors. They generally will not share with you these areas or behaviors that you could improve, unless you specially ask for their input in a constructive way toward wanting to improve yourself.

Getting yourself to see the picture is all about you taking the initiative to ask for feedback and not waiting for others to come forward with it. Anyway, if others come forward with feedback on their own, it is often not in a constructive way but more in a negative way. When they come with this type of feedback, then you are probably not in the right "mood" to listen to it anyway.

The best approach to see the picture is to ask one of your close friends or co-workers to help you with the areas or behaviors they think you could improve. Ask them for both your strengths and your weaknesses, and from their perspective, what would be the area or behaviors you should focus on for improvement. This advice could be valuable in helping you improve, grow, and become the person who can achieve the goals you have defined and to accomplish what you want with your life.

It is important to ask about both your strengths and weaknesses. Your strengths are what make you successful today. So, you should always be focussing on improving those weaknesses that will help you use your strengths even better. The more you are able to use your strengths, the more success you will be able achieve. Always focus first on those weaknesses that impact you using your strengths to the fullest.

Always focus first on those weaknesses that impact you using your strengths to the fullest.

So, if feedback from others will help you improve and grow faster, why don't you ask regularly for feedback from others? It is human nature to not want to hear negative things from others. You would not feel the encouragement to ask for this feedback.

However, you do see others who are constantly asking for feedback, and these are the people who are also successful, too. What is the trait that drives them to ask for this feedback and for others to not ask? Often, it comes down to the confidence that successful people have in themselves. They know that they will improve themselves faster by getting feedback from others, and that without feedback, they will never be able to take the action and improve on those "blind spots" in their behaviors. They understand that the more they improve, the more successful they can become.

It makes sense, doesn't it? So, the place to start is to build your confidence strong enough that it enables you to ask for the feedback from others. The people who get ahead in life and achieve success are constantly asking for feedback. They know that their success will only continue as long as they are growing, and the feedback will help them keep growing, and growing faster than without it.

Honest feedback always makes you better. Why not ask for feedback from others today?

- Ask trusted friends or co-workers for feedback.

- Understand both your strengths and your weaknesses.

- Focus your improvements on those weaknesses that impact you from using your strengths better.

TRUTH

38

Growth comes when you are comfortable being uncomfortable

Think back to all the occasions when you were doing something new for the first time. Were you feeling comfortable when you were first trying it? Probably not, if you are like everyone else. If you try new things you will be learning and growing, and also feeling a little uncomfortable.

Growth comes when you are trying to do something new or you experience new situations. However, you often try and avoid these new things because of the fear that you might not do it right the first time on behave in the right way.

People rarely do anything perfect the first time they try it. It makes perfect sense, but this is often forgotten when people avoid doing something because they think they might not do it right and might make a mistake. Think about this. If you are totally comfortable with what you are doing now, are you really challenging yourself and are you growing?

The successful people who get ahead in life are constantly challenging themselves to try new things and to attempt to do something they have never done before. They know that growth comes when they are moving forward and stretching themselves to use the abilities and the potential that they see inside them. Also, they know that they will make mistakes along the way, and that this is simply part of the learning process of trying something new—and especially in trying something new for the first time.

> If you are totally comfortable with what you are doing now, are you really challenging yourself and are you growing?

You could say that successful people have a goal to always being a little "uncomfortable." They believe that if they are totally comfortable with what they are doing, that they are not growing—that not growing will limit their future success. If you are always comfortable, are you growing?

Take the example of people who are afraid to speak in public. It is often said that this is one of the biggest fears in people's lives—to speak in public. What people are afraid of is being uncomfortable and possibly making a mistake. However, you could ask any successful speaker, and they could probably tell you that there were many times when they made mistakes in their speeches, but that did not stop them from being successful. In fact, it has been because of their drive to try new things and be uncomfortable at first (and make a few mistakes) that they have grown faster and became more successful. They didn't let being uncomfortable stop them from growing.

How about you? Are you totally comfortable in everything that you are doing today? Are you letting being uncomfortable stop you from growing?

Why not set a goal for yourself that you will always be trying something new in at least one part of your life each and every week. If you are trying something new in every part of your life all at once, this can be a little stressful and too much all at once. However, most people are trying almost nothing new and seem to live a life of "routine."

Take a look at your life today. Are there areas of your life where you are totally comfortable and have locked yourself into a routine? Take a good look at those areas and see what "uncomfortable" growth opportunities you have been avoiding, and focus yourself to take action on those opportunities this week. Remember, being a little uncomfortable equals growing.

Set the goal for yourself to get comfortable being a little uncomfortable, and you will always be growing and moving closer to the goals you have defined and what you want to accomplish in your life. Success comes faster when you are comfortable being a little uncomfortable.

> Set a goal for yourself that you will always be trying something new in at least one part of your life each week.

- Never be afraid to try something new and grow.

- Understand that no one does anything perfect the first time they try it.

- Become comfortable being a little uncomfortable.

TRUTH

Comparing yourself to others limits your growth

You often compare yourself to others. Some comparisons make you feel good, as you are thinking you are doing better than they are. Other comparisons make you feel bad, or at least make you feel that you could do more. However, all comparisons with others have a limit to the impact on you. The only comparison with no limit is comparing yourself to your potential.

Let's take a look at Tiger Woods. He and other people at the top of their sports are almost always comparing themselves to their potential—rather than to others. In the case of Tiger Woods, if he compared himself to others, he could then tend to relax a bit and slow down the development of his own golf game. In fact, Woods is one of the golfers who practices and works on his golf game the most, and he recently commented that there is a great deal of improvement he can make in his own golf game. Woods focuses on not comparing himself to others, but in comparing himself to the potential that he sees inside him.

> The only comparison with no limit is comparing yourself to your potential.

How about you? Do you compare yourself to others or to your potential? Everyone has different abilities, and success in life and getting things done is always about using those abilities to the fullest. Vince Lombardi said, "The measure of who we are is what we do with what we have." If you are like others, you have more within you than what you are currently using today.

Many people use their abilities to just get by. They have such a great potential within them, but instead of investing the time to develop that potential, they go on year after year just using it to live the life of just getting by. How about you? Are you developing the potential that is within you, or are you just using it to get by?

If you are like everyone else, you have within you the ability to accomplish more than what you are accomplishing today, and certainly more than what you think you can. Scientists say that humans only use a fraction of the abilities they have. With that being so, you, like everyone else, have the potential in you to accomplish a great deal more than what you are currently accomplishing.

The focus should never be on comparing yourself to others, but comparing yourself to your potential. In fact, most people have never even given thought to what that potential is. Have you? Why not invest the time to think through the potential that is inside you and how you can take action on leveraging it to get what you want (that success you have defined). The more you think about your potential, the more action you will take each and every day to use that potential.

By focusing on your potential and not on others, your only limiting factor in leveraging that potential to get what you want is just the belief in yourself that you can do it (and that's all within your control).

Remember, learn from others and their experiences, but never compare yourself to others. Focus your thoughts and energy on your potential. By focusing on your potential, you will grow to become the person who can achieve your goals and what you want to accomplish in your life.

- Compare yourself to your potential and not to others.

- Everyone has within himself or herself the potential for success.

- Only those who remind themselves of their potential will ever really use it.

Are you developing the potential that is within you, or are you just using it to get by?

TRUTH

40

Surround yourself with the *right* people to fuel your growth

You don't achieve success all by yourself. Also, you cannot learn enough or grow fast enough if you only rely on your own experiences to bring you this growth. You can read books and do your own personal development to help you grow, but you also need to meet and interact with people who will challenge your thinking and help you grow even faster.

Charlie Tremendous Jones said, "You will be the same five years from now except for two things: The books you read and the people you meet." You grow through your self-study, as well as through the people you meet and can learn from. To grow faster, you need to surround yourself with the right people who can help you grow. Are the people you surround yourself with today helping you grow?

Think about the people you meet on a daily and weekly basis in both your professional and personal life. Are these people helping you grow to become the person you would like to be? Are they helping you achieve the success you would like to achieve? And, lastly, are they helping your find enjoyment and fulfilment on the journey toward that success you desire?

> You also need to meet and interact with people who will challenge your thinking.

These are great questions to ask yourself. If you are like others, your success might be slowed down by the people you surround yourself with the most. That sounds a little negative, but if you think about it; you can see how that may be true.

You surround yourself with people who make you feel comfortable, and that's especially true for your personal life. You want to feel relaxed around the people you are with. However, you grow most when you are uncomfortable. If this is true, keeping the same people around you all the time is probably slowing your growth. If your growth is being slowed, then you can imagine that the pace to reach your goals and what you want is being slowed as well.

You can see the impact of surrounding yourself with right people on the lives of today's successful people.

Everyone knows of the American Idol's Simon Cowell. If you were to ask Simon about the people who helped make him a success, he would probably mention the name Pete Waterman. Early in Simon's career, he followed Pete Waterman around and learned a great deal about the music business from him. This could probably be described as a foundation for his success.

Let's take another example. Look at Tony Robbins, the motivational speaker, and someone who has made an impact on millions of lives. When Tony was younger, he worked for another great speaker—Jim Rohn. Again, if you asked Tony about the people who helped shape his thinking and helped him succeed, he would mention Jim Rohn's name.

Both Simon Cowell and Tony Robbins chose to be around people that they could learn from and who could help them grow. Who could you invest more time in getting closer to and be around for you to grow faster as well?

There's an old saying, "Your network creates your net worth." Whom you know and spend the most time with is one of the most powerful indicators of your future success and net worth. Given the success you have defined for yourself and the goals that will help drive you to reach it, don't you think one of the most important actions for you to take is in defining who can help you grow and reach your goals faster?

Invest a few minutes today and think about what types of people and who specifically could help you the most. When you have this list, think about the possible ways to put yourself in a better position to meet these people and to get to know them better. This could be through formal networks and by utilizing the people you already know.

> **Whom you know and spend the most time with is one of the most powerful indicators of your future success and net worth.**

The truth is, if you haven't defined who can help you the most, you will never take the necessary actions to put yourself in a position to meet them. Surround yourself with people who will help you grow.

- Take a look at the people with whom you spend most of your time.

- Are the people around you helping you grow as fast as you would like to?

- Your network creates your net worth.

TRUTH

41

Pride in what you do creates excellence in what you do

Think back in your life, and you will find a time when you did an exceptional job on a particular assignment, whether it was during your school days or in your work. If you think about it, you will most likely find that you took great pride in what you accomplished, and that pride was most likely the reason you did it so well in the first place.

For you to get things done, the same drive for quality and pride in your work can drive you to accomplish great things. Pride always gets driven by the commitment you have behind what you are doing, as commitment drives ownership.

You see the difference pride makes when you consider how you treat your own car versus a rental car. Whenever you rent a car, you often don't take care of the car, as you would have your own. You probably don't wash it when it is dirty, as you will probably only make use of it for a very short time. You just don't have the pride of ownership and take care of the car as if it were your own.

> **Pride always gets driven by the commitment you have behind what you are doing, as commitment drives ownership.**

However, could you envision a time when you might take pride in that rental car and treat it more as if it were your own? What if you had rented this car for business and were using it to visit customers. If the car were dirty, would that have given a good impression to the customers you were visiting? In this particular case, you would probably wash the car before visiting your customers, as you have now taken some pride in being able to make a good impression on your customers.

Pride in what you do is more about how you go about your day-to-day activities than about any big initiatives or changes you could make. It is about always looking to do your best on what you could call "the fundamentals." These are usually all the common activities you do during your day. However, the people who take "pride" in their work always do these common activities to the best of their abilities.

How you do these common activities, day in and day out, is what will always provide the foundation of your success. The foundation of success is doing the necessary, when it is necessary, and always doing it to the best of your abilities.

People who take "pride" in their work always do common activities to the best of their abilities.

In today's world, too many people are constantly acting as if good enough is good enough. When you don't have the pride in your work, you always seem to do only the minimum and often to just produce acceptable quality that's good enough. However, if you keep repeating this way of working, the quality associated with good enough always seems to get lower and lower. Whenever you settle for good enough, you will tend to settle for less in the future. It is as if you are constantly lowering your standards as long as someone isn't complaining. However, at the same time you are constantly lowering the "pride" you have in your own work.

People who have pride in their work will always strive to produce their best, and it is only by focusing on doing your best, that you keep your "pride" strong. How about you? Are you always striving to do your best in all situations and circumstances?

Remember, pride in doing the necessary when it is necessary will help you get things done, today and every day—and always done to the best of your abilities.

- Doing your best *will* always create pride in your work.

- When you have pride in your work, you always accomplish more.

- Building the commitment creates ownership, and ownership creates the pride.

TRUTH

42

It is all about making common sense common practice

In all the Truths you have read, you probably didn't see any earth-shattering concepts, tools, or techniques to improve getting more things done. That's interesting, isn't it? However, what you did read were many common sense ideas that all successful people have used to get things done and achieve success over the years—and as far back as history shows.

What you get done and accomplish in your life does not depend on coming up with fantastic ideas every day and doing something different. It comes down to taking the necessary *common sense* actions and having the discipline to actually keep doing them—day in and day out.

You cannot hit a target you do not have.

Many people lack the discipline to implement the habits that make common sense common practice. These actions are always easy to do, and there's nothing that requires you to have a Ph.D. to do them. However, because these actions are so easy to do, they are also easy not to do.

You have read many truths that talk about how to get things done by yourself and along with others, and these have covered many areas. However, you could summarize what you have learned to just a couple of common sense actions.

- Defining what you want? Success

- Deciding what you need to do on a daily and weekly basis to get it? Discipline

Common sense says that you cannot hit a target you do not have.

If you want to be great at getting the *right* things done, you have to start by defining clearly what you want and why you want it.

Also, common sense says that you cannot get different results by doing the same things.

You probably already know what you should be doing on a daily and weekly basis to get what you want. Right? If you are like others, *the problem is never in the knowing, only in the doing.*

Take some of the ideas from the other truths and make the decision to put those daily and weekly habits in your life starting today. No one can do this for you, and no on knows what you want, and why you want it more than you. Jim Rohn says it best, "You can't hire someone else to do your push ups for you." It is simply a decision you need to make, and then make a commitment to yourself to take the necessary actions that are behind that decision.

What common sense do you need to make common practice today?

Pick one common sense habit that would move you closer to the success you want and the life you want to live. Create a plan of action that will ensure you make the habit a real habit. If what you want is so important to you and the *why* is so big that you have to have it, then it will be much easier for you to keep that commitment to yourself and create that habit.

In *The Truth About Getting More Thing Done*, you have realized that it is almost always about you, your focus, and the discipline behind that focus. It is not about any particular tool or time-management technique. You want to get things done for a purpose, achieving something you want, versus just ticking off completed tasks.

Here's a word to remember, and three key points that utilize the letters in the word. It summaries a great approach to get you started.

The word is *WHY!*

1. **W**hat success do you **W**ant and **W**hy do you want it?
2. **H**ow can you get it done (the outcomes and your **H**abits) and what **H**elp do you need from others?
3. Who do **Y**ou need to become and what discipline do **Y**ou need to put into creating the daily and weekly habits that will enable you to get it done and achieve the success you desire.

Make common sense common practice—which is the uncommon thing to do!

References

The keyword enclosed in parentheses at the end of each entry highlights the subject related to the reference.

Truth 1

Les Brown. *Step into Your Greatness Live*, www.tstn.com (Potential)

Brian Tracy. *Brian Tracy Success Mastery Academy*, Strategic Marketing Group, 1998 (Clarity)

Nido Qubein, www.nidoqubein.com (Future)

Truth 2

George Zalucki. *An Experience to Make a Difference*, www.georgezalucki.com, 1992 (Why and Desire)

Truth 3

Les Brown. *Step into Your Greatness—Live*, www.tstn.com (Belief)

Denis Waitley. *Winners Believe with Passion*, www.tstn.com (Belief)

Truth 4

Brian Tracy. *Brian Tracy Success Mastery Academy*, Strategic Marketing Group, 1998 (Focus)

Stan Christensen. Stanford University—Entrepreneurial Thought Leader Podcasts, http://edcorner.stanford.edu/authorMaterialInfo.html?author=211 (Criteria)

Truth 5

Brian Tracy. *Brian Tracy Success Mastery Academy*, Strategic Marketing Group, 1998 (Focus)

Truth 6

Brian Tracy. *Brian Tracy Success Mastery Academy*, Strategic Marketing Group, 1998 (Clarity)

Truth 7

Brian Tracy. *Brian Tracy Success Mastery Academy*, Strategic Marketing Group, 1998 (Goals)

Dr. Maxwell Maltz. www.psycho-cybernetics.com/maltz.html (Thought)

Robert H. Schuller. Crystal Cathedral, www.crystalcathedral.org (Thought)

Truth 8

Jim Rohn. *The Art of Exceptional Living*, Nightingale-Conant, 2003 (Journey)

Earl Nightingale. http://earlnightingale.com (Belief)

Denis Waitley. *Winners Determine Their Futures*, www.tstn.com (Future)

Truth 9

David Allen. *Getting Things Done: The Art of Stress-Free Productivity*, Penguin, 2002 (Follow-Up)

Bill Creech. *The Five Pillars of TQM*, Dutton Adult, 1995 (Ownership)

Truth 10

Les Brown. *Step into Your Greatness Live*, www.tstn.com (Belief)

George Zalucki. *Emotions—Servants or Destroyers*, www.georgezalucki.com, 1992 (Belief)

Bob Proctor. *Getting to Know You*, www.tstn.com (Paradigms)

Truth 11

Jim Rohn. *The Art of Exceptional Living*, Nightingale-Conant, 2003 (Today)

John Wooden. *Wooden*, McGraw-Hill, 1997 (Today)

Truth 12

Dan Lier. *America's Coach: Your True Potential*, www.tstn.com (Belief)

Les Brown. *Step into Your Greatness Live*, www.tstn.com (Belief)

Truth 13

Zig Ziglar. *See You at the Top*, Pelican Publishing Company; 2nd Revised edition, 2000 (Attitude)

Rick Pitino. *Lead to Succeed: 10 Traits of Great Leadership in Business and Life*, Broadway, 2001 (Choice)

Truth 14

James Allen. *As a Man Thinketh*, www.asamanthinketh.net/JamesAllen.htm (Thoughts)

Brian Tracy. *Brian Tracy Success Mastery Academy*, Strategic Marketing Group, 1998 (Thoughts)

David Allen. *Getting Things Done: The Art of Stress-Free Productivity*, Penguin, 2002 (Next Action)

Truth 15

Jerry Clark. *Think Like a Giant*, www.tstn.com (Thoughts)

Truth 16

Jim Rohn. *The Art of Exceptional Living*, Nightingale-Conant, 2003 (Action)

Truth 17

David Allen. *Getting Things Done: The Art of Stress-Free Productivity*, Penguin, 2002 (Think Ahead, Rapid Refocusing)

Truth 18

David Allen. *Getting Things Done: The Art of Stress-Free Productivity*, Penguin, 2002 (Think Ahead)

Rick Pitino. *Lead to Succeed: 10 Traits of Great Leadership in Business and Life*, Broadway, 2001 (Prepare)

Truth 19

Les Brown. *Step into Your Greatness Live*, www.tstn.com (Action)

George Zalucki. *Emotions—Servants or Destroyers*, www.georgezalucki.com, 1992 (Action)

Truth 20

John Wooden. *Wooden*, McGraw-Hill, 1997 (Today)

Truth 21

Jim Rohn. *The Art of Exceptional Living*, Nightingale-Conant, 2003 (Discipline)

Jim Cathcart. *The Purpose of Selling*, www.tstn.com

Truth 22

Brad Isaac. *Jerry Seinfeld's Productivity Secret*, www. fromedwardwithlove.com/jerry-seinfelds-productivity-secret (Daily Discipline)

Truth 23

Brian Tracy. *Brian Tracy Success Mastery Academy*, Strategic Marketing Group, 1998 (Extra)

Truth 24

Jim Rohn. *The Art of Exceptional Living*, Nightingale-Conant, 2003 (Action)

Truth 25

Denis Waitley. *The Psychology of Winning*, Abridged Edition, Nightingale-Conant, 2005 (Habits)

Truth 26

Tony Alessandra. *The Platinum Rule*, www.tstn.com (Adaptability)

Truth 27

George Zalucki. *Emotions—Servants or Destroyers*, www. georgezalucki.com, 1992 (Listen)

Truth 28

Jeffrey Gitomer. *Little Red Book of Selling*, 1st Edition, Bard Press, 2004 (Sales)

Zig Ziglar. *See You at the Top*, Pelican Publishing Company; 2nd Revised edition, 2000 (Sales)

Truth 29

Larry Bossidy, Ram Charan, Charles Burck, *Execution: The Discipline of Getting Things Done*, Crown Business, 1st Edition, 2002 (Questions)

Jack Welch and John A. Byrne. *Jack: Straight from the Gut*, Business Plus, 2003 (Questions)

Truth 30
Jim Rohn. *The Art of Exceptional Living*, Nightingale-Conant, 2003 (Stories)

Truth 31
David Allen. *Getting Things Done: The Art of Stress-Free Productivity*, Penguin, 2002 (Communication)

Truth 32
Jeffrey Gitomer. *Little Red Book of Selling*, 1st Edition, Bard Press, 2004 (Listen)

Connie Podesta. *Life Would Be Easy If It Weren't for Other People*, Pelican Publishing Company, 2nd revised edition, 2000 (Listen)

Truth 33
Tony Alessandra. *The Platinum Rule*, www.tstn.com (Adaptability)

Zig Ziglar. www.ziglar.com (Serve)

Truth 35
Patrick M. Lencioni. *The Five Dysfunctions of a Team: A Leadership Fable*, 1st edition, Jossey-Boss, 2002 (Trust, Conflict)

Patrick M. Lencioni. Leadership TRAQ Podcast, www.leadershiptraq.com/podcast/traqpod.html (Trust)

Truth 36
David Allen. *Getting Things Done: The Art of Stress-Free Productivity*, Penguin, 2002 (Follow-Up)

Patrick M. Lencioni. Leadership TRAQ Podcast, www.leadershiptraq.com/podcast/traqpod.html (Trust)

Larry Bossidy, Ram Charan, Charles Burck. *Execution: The Discipline of Getting Things Done*, Crown Business, 1st Edition, 2002 (Follow-up)

Truth 37

Les Brown. *Step into Your Greatness Live*, www.tstn.com (Potential)

Marcus Buckingham and Curt Coffman. *First Break All the Rules: What the World's Greatest Managers Do Differently*, 1st Edition, Simon & Schuster, 1999 (Strengths)

Truth 38

George Zalucki. *Emotions—Servants or Destroyers*, www.george-zalucki.com, 1992 (Uncomfortable)

Steve Siebold. *Developing Mental Toughness Skills*, www.tstn.com (Thoughts)

Truth 39

Vince Lombardi. www.vincelombardi.com/about/highlights.htm (Potential)

Dan Lier. America's Coach: *Your True Potential*, www.tstn.com (Potential)

Truth 40

Charlie "Tremendous" Jones. www.executivebooks.com/cjones (Network)

Les Brown. *Step into Your Greatness Live*, www.tstn.com (Potential)

Steve Young. Stanford University—Entrepreurial Thought Leader Podcasts, http://edcorner.stanford.edu/authorMaterialInfo. html?mid=1739 (Trust)

Truth 41

Bill Creech. *The Five Pillars of TQM*, Dutton Adult, 1995 (Ownership)

Truth 42

Jim Rohn. *The Art of Exceptional Living*, Nightingale-Conant, 2003 (Discipline)

Acknowledgments

No one can accomplish anything without the inspiration and help of others, and this book is no exception. Whatever we accomplish in life is enabled by the strong foundation of what we have learned from others. A strong foundation of information, insights, and ideas brings us more inspiration, energy, and creativity to Get More Done.

The information, ideas, and insights of Brian Tracy, Les Brown, David Allen, Zig Ziglar, General Bill Creech, George Zalucki, Jeffery Gitomer, Jerry Clark, Dan Lier, Denis Waitley, Tony Alesandra, Jim Rohn, Jack Welch, and John Wooden have all helped over the years to create a strong foundation from which this book was inspired.

Lastly to my wife, Atsuko, for all her support and encouragement.

About the Author

Mark Fritz is the founder of Procedor, a company focused on two main areas: Personal Effectiveness *(Leading Yourself)* and Leadership Effectiveness *(Leading Others)*. Mark provides consulting, training, and coaching/mentoring services to companies throughout the world. Mark has lived in the U.S., Singapore, Egypt, the Netherlands, Italy, Japan, and the UK, and has successfully combined best practices from around the world to create an innovative set of business tools and insights that can help businesses of all sizes be even more successful.

He is an associate of Ashridge College in the UK, co-teaching Leading Complex Teams, and a visiting professor teaching Virtual Leadership at the HEC in France, at the Instituto de Empresa in Spain, and at IFL—Stockholm School of Economics in Sweden. Mark's natural charm and personable style, enhanced by a great sense of humor, has made him a speaker of choice at company events and seminars. He is an affiliate of the prestigious CSA Celebrity Speakers and regularly speaks on Personal Effectiveness for Leaders and Virtual Leadership (Leading People at a Distance).

Mark is also the author of *Time to Get Started*, a compilation of his best daily thoughts from the first 18 months of writing. You can read Mark's Daily Thoughts at www.procedor.com/daily-thought.

Visit Mark at www.procedor.com.

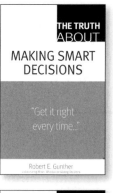